assisi Community

BEYOND SERVANTHOOD

Christianity and the Liberation of Women

Susan Nelson Dunfee

D1602638

UNIVERSITY
PRESS OF
AMERICA

Lanham • New York • London

Copyright © 1989 by

University Press of America,® Inc.

4720 Boston Way
Lanham, MD 20706

3 Henrietta Street
London WC2E 8LU England

Printed in the United States of America

British Cataloging in Publication Information Available

Library of Congress Cataloging-in-Publication Data

Dunfee, Susan Nelson, 1947–
Beyond servanthood : Christianity and the liberation of women /
Susan Nelson Dunfee.
    p. cm.
Bibliography: p.
1. Women in Christianity. 2. Patriarchy—Religious aspects—
Christianity. 3. Feminism—Religious aspects—Christianity.
4. Ser vice (Theology) 5. Altruism. I. Title.
BV639.W7D86   1988
208'.8042—dc 19   88–27856 CIP
ISBN 0–8191–7223–5 (alk. paper)
ISBN 0–8191–7224–3 (pbk. : alk. paper)

ACKNOWLEDGMENTS

I could not have written this book without the help of many people. The community of women in Claremont has been an important support to me in my journey. Thiasos, formerly Claremont Women in Religion, first encouraged me to pursue my intuitions and challenged me to make a feminist perspective the focus of my work; Catherine Keller repeatedly amazed me with possibilities for a different reality; Nelle Morton encouraged me to be myself; Ann Taves revealed to me what feminist sparking can be all about; Jane Dempsey Douglass was a crucial touchstone in my exploration of feminism within the Church; Regina Mooney blessed me with her vibrant energy and helped me to discover some of my own; and Earlynne Biering was a constant friend, supporting me through my ups and downs.

Several women in the United Presbyterian Church in Southern California also were an important source of support. I'd like to thank particularly Jean Vieten, Jerry Rodiwald, Sue Naumann and Sylvia Karcher for listening to me and affirming my work--and Ann Hayman, whose ministry to women who want "off the street" convinced me again of the importance of the movement for women's liberation in general and my thesis, in particular.

The people of the Village Presbyterian Church in Arcadia, California, also were a special support. To Jim and Janette Seright, the folks at Westminster Gardens, Marion McMillan and Gussie Betzold I give an extra thanks.

And I thank my doctoral committee at Claremont Graduate School: Marjorie Suchocki, who first breathed the words "graduate school" into my inner ear; Dan Roades, in whose class my vision first cleared; Joe Hough, who consistently engaged me in critical dialogue; Jack Verheyden, who has been a loyal friend and teacher and who "stepped in" when he was needed; and John Cobb, whose patient and persistent hearing literally heard me into my own speech. John has been a special adviser, influencing me through his life, work and ability to listen deeply, challenging me to be a <u>Christian</u> feminist theologian, yet allowing me the "space" to follow my own journey--to speak with integrity from my own center.

iii

I would also like to acknowledge the following
as well: Beacon Press for permission to reprint from
both Beyond God the Father by Mary Daly--Copyright
1973 by Mary Daly, and Gyn/Ecology by Mary
Daly--Copyright 1978 by Mary Daly; Alfred A. Knopf,
Inc. for permission to reprint from The Second Sex by
Simone de Beauvoir; World Council of Churches
Publications, Geneva, Switzerland for permission to
quote from The Community of Women and Men in the
Church, edited by Constance F. Parvey; University
Press of America, Inc. for permission to reprint from
Sex, Sin and Grace by Judith Plaskow; Judson Press
for permission to reprint from A Different Heaven and
Earth by Sheila Collins; The Prilgrim Press for
permission to reprint from Beyond Mere Obedience by
Dorothee Soelle--Copyright 1982 by The Pilgrim Press;
Harvard Univerity Press for permission to reprint
from In a Different Voice by Carol Gilligan; The
University of California Press for permission to
reprint from The Reproduction of Motherhood by Nancy
Chodorow; Abingdon Press for permission to reprint
from The Interpreter's Bible vol. VIII; Wm. B.
Eerdmans Publishing Co. for permission to reprint
from Theological Dictionary of the New Testament,
Vol. II--Copyright 1964 by Wm. B. Eerdmans Publishing
Co.; Harper & Row Publishers, Inc. for permission to
reprint from God's Grace and Man's Hope by Daniel Day
Williams, and from The Power of the Powerless by
Jürgen Moltmann; Fortress Press for permission to
reprint from Liberty, Equality, Sisterhood by
Elisabeth Moltmann-Wendel, and from The Passion for
Life by Jürgen Moltmann; The University of Chicago
Press for permission to reprint from "The Human
Situation: A Feminine View" by Valerie Saivings
Goldstein found in Journal of Religion, 40; Orbis
Books for permission to reprint from To Set at
Liberty by Delwin Brown; Oxford University Press for
permission to reprint from Love, Power and Justice by
Paul Tillich; Anne Wilson Schaef for permission to
reprint from Women's Reality; Jean Baker Miller for
permission to reprint from Toward a New Psychology of
Women; Catherine Keller for permission to reprint
from From a Broken Web; The Crossroad Publishing
Company for permission to reprint from In Memory of
Her: A Feminist Theological Reconstruction of
Christian Origins by Elisabeth Schüssler
Fiorenza--Copyright 1983 by Elisabeth Schüssler
Fiorenza; The MacMillan Publishing Company for
permission to reprint from The Nature and Destiny of
Man vols. 1 and 2 by Reinhold Niebuhr--volume 1

     And finally, I thank Mike Dunfee; Iris Lowe who
not only typed and edited the manuscript, but paid me
the supreme compliment of hearing what I had to say;
Ronald Stone who encouraged me to send the manuscript
to University Press of America; Carol Pitts and
Beverly Mosley who dialogued with me; Ulrich Mauser
who made adjustments so that the manuscript could be
typed; and C. Samuel Calian who prodded me on.

TABLE OF CONTENTS

INTRODUCTION

The question about which this book is concerned first was formed in the spring of 1979 when, as a seminarian, I was part of a planning committee that invited Mary Daly to Pittsburgh Theological Seminary to address the question: "Can one be Christian and feminist, too?" Although Daly accepted the invitation of our committee, when it came time for her to address our conference, it became obvious that she had no intention of addressing the question at all. Beginning by noting that it was as impossible to talk about being Christian and feminist as it was impossible to be healthy and have cancer, she proceeded to lead us on a gyn/ecological journey into the other-world of women's spirituality.

As I realized during that conference, for Daly, Christianity and feminism contradict each other. Christianity, as she makes clear in her Gyn/Ecology,[1] is but one manifestation of the major religion of the planet: patriarchy. As such, it is not about the empowerment of women into our own liberation, but exists on stolen women's energy. Christianity is all about keeping women in our patriarchal place.

In the years since first being confronted by Mary Daly, I have valued her critique of Christianity and have found her exploration into the nature of feminist spirituality personally empowering. However, I have also come to realize that my experience of Christianity is not hers. Although I, too, have experienced sexism within the Christian church (the patriarchal powers that be have been resistant to change) and have known the oppressive nature of Christian symbolism, I also must honestly say that I have experienced encouragement and appreciation for the type of questions that I have asked. Moreover, I have been impressed by the great influx of women into Protestant seminaries, where we are being admitted, and by our enthusiasm for becoming Christian ministers. While I cannot begin to explain the phenomenon in its complexity, it at least has led me to ask whether women have found something encouraging and empowering in Christian experience that has led us into preparation for the Christian ministry. It is possible, of course, that these women are not "feminist" or that we are merely "passing through" on our feminist journeys beyond

Christianity. But I also have been impressed by what I have heard from several homiletics professors in these seminaries. It appears that women are not only attending seminaries in greater numbers, but we also are becoming the better preachers. Moreover, as one professor suggested to me, we are preaching in a new way, a way this professor could not quite explain. As I have considered this phenomenon, it appears to me that women are preaching in a new way because we are preaching from our own experience, an experience that has not been included in most preaching, from our own stories. This suggests to me that women are speaking within Christianity in our own voices.

These questionings and observations have led me, several years later, to raise the question again--but this time to myself: Can one be Christian and feminist, too? However, now I am asking the question in a different form. Concerned with more than whether it is possible for a woman to reconcile her Christianity with her feminism, I now ask: Can Christianity empower women to experience our own liberation? Such Christian feminists as Elisabeth Moltmann-Wendel, Elisabeth Schüssler Fiorenza, Rosemary Radford Ruether, among others, have suggested that there is in Christianity an intent to liberation that basically resonates with the feminist movement's call for women to be liberated from patriarchy.[2] The purpose of this book is to consider this intuition in the context of women's experience to determine whether Christianity really can empower women to our liberation.

Since I am concerned about whether Christianity can empower women to our own liberation, I have chosen to begin this book with an exploration of women's experience.[3] The liberation that Christianity offers must meet women's experience of bondage and women's intuition of what liberation is all about if it truly can be said to empower women's liberation. Chapter I explores women's bondage, our process of liberation, and the ways in which we understand our liberation. This chapter provides the criteria by which we can judge whether Christianity can empower women to be liberated--whether Christianity can empower women to speak in our own voices.

In Chapter II we consider the arguments of Rosemary Radford Ruether and Elisabeth Schüssler

Fiorenza that Christianity can be a force for the empowerment of women today. Schüssler-Fiorenza's work, In Memory of Her,[4] is a reconstruction of Christian origins that, in faithfulness to Christian texts, puts women in the center of Christian history. Her work is a key one in such a consideration of Christianity for two reasons. First, it is one of the most recent books available on the subject. Secondly, it attempts to take into account the argument between what Carol P. Christ and Judith Plaskow[5] have characterized as the "reformist" branch of the feminist spirituality movement, which seeks to reform Christianity and other patriarchal religions, and the "revolutionary" one, which argues that these religions are patriarchal to the core. Chapter II asks the question whether Christianity is necessarily patriarchal. It seeks an answer by exploring Rosemary Ruether's argument that the prophetic-messianic tradition is usable for women's liberation, and Schüssler-Fiorenza's reconstruction of Christian origins that characterizes the early Christian community as a community of equals in which all were liberated from patriarchal forms of domination and submission--a community that, she says, was characterized by service and altruism--placing the needs of others and the community first.

Chapter III takes the theological symbols of service and altruism and returns to women's experience to test their liberating potential. Schüssler-Fiorenza has argued that solidarity with the history of women in early Christianity can empower women today. I ask in this chapter whether the theological symbols of service and altruism that emerge out of that history can in fact function as symbols for women's liberation. Even if the God of Christianity and the teaching of Jesus point to a liberating intent at the center of Christianity, a problem remains. If the nature of the redeemed community, the character of the state of liberation, is not liberating to women, then the intent is not fulfilled, and Christianity cannot empower women today. To ask whether liberation characterized by service and altruism can be liberating to women, Chapter III explores some of the recent work done on the nature of women's development into full, liberating selfhood. Because feminists insist that women's experience is not the same as what patriarchal society has considered to be "human" experience, we first must explore the nature of this different experience before we can determine whether the ideals of service and altruism can be empowering for women today in our liberation process. In Chapter III, I argue that they cannot.

Rather than terminating the discussion with this discovery, in Chapter IV I explore the intention behind the affirmation that the Christian community, the community of those liberated to their human wholeness, is characterized by service and altruism. Service and altruism may mean bondage and self-negation and not liberation for women. But we still can ask whether this is the intent of the call for service and altruism. To answer this question, I will turn to theologians Reinhold Niebuhr, Daniel Day Williams and Paul Tillich--all well-known for their writings on Christian love--to discover the presuppositions regarding the self behind each man's work.[6] In doing so, I am seeking to determine whether the sacrifice--or negation--of the self is necessary. I have chosen to begin with Reinhold Niebuhr because he uses the language of sacrificial love and self-sacrifice in his discussion of love. Williams, in his argument for _mutuality_ in love, offers another approach that counters Niebuhr's. What interests me for the purpose of this project is that while Niebuhr and Williams have taken different positions on the character of love, they both assume a _self_ that is to _do_ the loving. Tillich's work is of interest because he makes clear both that love assumes there are separate selves to be reunited through love and that something other than love makes this selfhood possible. Thus, by exploring the positions of these three theologians, I argue that the human experience to which Christianity calls people--one to be characterized by service and altruism--is dipolar: one that affirms _both_ the self _and_ the nature of that self as open to _the_ needs and concerns of others. Moreover, within the context of this re-exploration into the nature of service and altruism, I question not only the intent behind the call to service and altruism, but also the adequacy of service and altruism to characterize a community that is both composed of those who have been liberated from oppression to a new fullness of opportunity and that is intent upon mediating this liberation to the world around it. I argue that service and altruism are not adequate and that we need to move beyond service and altruism--beyond servanthood--to find a more adequate way to characterize the Christian experience and call it into being.

Having explored the dimensions of service and altruism and questioned their adequacy to interpret the Christian experience of liberation, I explore in Chapter V the Christian experience of liberation through the theological symbol of freedom. Jesus, it is affirmed in Scripture,[7] came to set at liberty the oppressed; Paul has said that in Christ we are free; Elisabeth Schüssler Fiorenza has reconstructed an early Christian community where people were freed from patriarchal patterns of submission to participate in a community known for its egalitarian nature--a community where no one had power over another, where each served the other, and where Christ's concern for solidarity with the oppressed was lived out. Chapter V asks: What is the nature of this freedom? Does this freedom contradict the insistence that the liberation experienced in Christianity is one characterized by service and altruism? And, finally, can this notion of freedom empower women to our own liberation--to speak in our own voices?

To answer these questions I turn to the work of several theologians (Rudolf Bultmann, Dorothee Soelle, Delwin Brown, Jürgen Moltmann) who have characterized the life of freedom in Christ--and to my own exegetical word study of the "no longer do I call you slaves but friends" passage of John 15. By examining the tension between friendship and slavery in this passage, I argue that Jesus' intent is in fact to call people to be a community of friends who are not to be slaves to one another but who are freed to respond to one another's needs "in their own voices." Thus I conclude that it is freedom--and the authority and friendship that freedom in Christ entail--that better characterizes the experience of Christian liberation and that in fact can call it into being.

The intent of this project is not to whitewash Christianity of its misogynist traditions. This is not a refutation of the very real culpability Christianity bears for the perpetuation of women's bondage to patriarchy and the alienation of women from ourselves. As Charlene Spretnak has pointed

out,[8]   Christianity   still   is   used   against   the
movement for women's liberation.   The hope of this
book is twofold.   If Christianity can empower women
to our liberation today, this book seeks to make that
power available to women in our journeys.   And, if
women can be empowered by Christianity, this book
attempts to reclaim Christianity for the work of
liberation from those who would use it to reinforce
patriarchal systems of submission and oppression.

[1]Mary Daly, Gyn/Ecology: The Metaethics of Radical Feminism (Boston: Beacon Press, 1978), see in particular the "Prelude to the first passage," pp. 37-42.

[2]All of these women have published several books and/or articles on this subject. See especially: Elisabeth Moltmann-Wendel and Jürgen Moltmann, "Becoming Human in New Community," in The Community of Women and Men in the Church, ed., Constance F. Parvey (Philadelphia: Fortress Press, 1983), pp. 29-42; Elisabeth Schüssler Fiorenza, In Memory of Her: A Feminist Reconstruction of Christian Origins (New York: Crossroad, 1983); Rosemary Radford Ruether, Sexism and God-Talk: Toward a Feminist Theology (Boston: Beacon Press, 1983).

[3]Because the works cited in this text have been written by white, western women about the experience of white, Western women in a patriarchal society, this book is more correctly about white, Western women's liberation.

[4]Schüssler-Fiorenza, In Memory of Her, see note 2.

[5]Carol P. Christ and Judith Plaskow, "Introduction," WomanSpirit Rising (New York: Harper & Row, 1979), Christ and Plaskow editors, p. 10.

[6]In moving to some of the theological literature on love, I am assuming a certain correlation between service and altruism--meaning placing the needs of others and the community first--and love. I am dependent upon Elisabeth Schüssler Fiorenza's equation of altruism with love (see note #105 on p. 70) and upon Reinhold Niebuhr's understanding of the "law of love" as the transcendent opening up of the self to live vulnerably "in and for others," to make this correlation. See p. 106-107 of this manuscript.

[7]Luke 4:18-21.

[8]Charlene Spretnak, "The Christian Right's 'Holy War' Against Feminism," The Politics of Women's Spirituality (Garden City, New York: Anchor Books,

1982), edited by Charlene Spretnak, pp. 470-96.

CHAPTER I

To Speak in Our Own Voices

The purpose of this book is to answer the question whether Christianity can empower women to experience liberation today. In order to answer this question, it is first necessary to determine what women mean by liberation. From what are women seeking liberation? How do women describe the liberated experience? And, how do women understand the process toward liberation?

This chapter shall explore these questions through the writings of various feminist thinkers in order to formulate the criteria by which we can judge whether or not Christianity can empower women's liberation as women understand it. Once we have established the criteria, we can begin to explore in subsequent chapters whether or not Christianity can in fact empower women to be liberated.

When women speak of our need for liberation we point to our bondage. Patriarchy, we argue, has self-consciously kept women in bondage for centuries. Whether through actual foot binding, gynecological mutilation, or the rules and pressures of social convention,[1] women have been confined by patriarchal societies to positions of subordination--positions that have cut us off from our full human potential.

Simone de Beauvoir gives us our first clue as to the nature of this bondage. Writing at the beginning of the contemporary "wave" of the feminist movement, de Beauvoir recognizes that women have been denied our full human freedom and transcendence because we have been forced by men in a patriarchal society to be objects, things that are packaged and defined. She says:

> . . . what peculiarly signalizes the situation of woman is that she--a free and autonomous being like all human creatures-- nevertheless finds herself living in a world where men compel her to assume the status of the Other. They propose to stabilize her as object and to doom her to immanence since her transcendence is to be over-shadowed and forever transcended by

1

another ego . . . which is essential and
sovereign.[2]

As de Beauvoir states it, women have lost our
transcendence, our freedom to be subjects, ones who
create and define. We have been reduced to what she
calls a state of immanence--consigned to a repetition
of what women have always been supposed to be: Woman.

And what is this Woman that women are supposed
to become? Woman, de Beauvoir asserts, is the model
according to which patriarchy molds women. She is
the form that keeps women confined. She is the
example according to which women are denied the
freedom to be fully human--to be ones who define
ourselves. She, "has ovaries, a uterus; these
peculiarities imprison her in her subjectivity,
circumscribe her within the limits of her own
nature."[3] Rather than defining "herself by dealing
with nature on her own account in her emotional
life,"[4] Woman is defined by nature. Her anatomy is
her destiny. As biological being, Woman is destined
to be the "victim of the species," limited, to her
anatomical functioning as mother. She thus has been
denied any options that would allow her to affirm her
biological functions in another way (which would be
an expression of her full humanity). Defined by
nature, she is denied the opportunity to define
herself.

But women, de Beauvoir argues, have been
confined by more than definition according to our
biological destiny, for Woman is also "simply what
man decrees."[5] "She is not regarded as an
autonomous being."[6] She is not allowed to define
herself "in herself." Rather, "she is defined and
differentiated with reference to man and not he with
reference to her; she is the incidental, the
inessential as opposed to the essential. He is the
Subject, he is the Absolute--she is the Other."[7]
As the Other, she has borne the names assigned to her
by men and her very existence has been understood to
be tied to her relationship to men.

Whereas the role of Other, as de Beauvoir has
asserted, has constrained women within sexually
stereotypical roles--those determined by nature and
our relationships to men--it has confined us as well
to those attributes the male has wished to project
upon us. As Jürgen Moltmann has described the

process:

>Patriarchy cut the male in half. It split him into a subject, consisting of reason and will, and an object, consisting of heart, feelings, and physical needs. He had to identify with the former and keep his distance from the latter. This isolated the male and brought about a certain self-hatred. This division in the male is reflected and takes an aggressive form in the male subjugation and domination of supposedly "frail," "emotional," and "physical" women. [8]

While the male, as Subject, is named superior and rational, women have been stereotyped by and confined within the attributes of "frail," "emotional," and "physical." Patriarchal men, not wishing to be identified with these traits, assign them to women, and then name them as inferior and treat the women who bear them as objects of contempt. [9]

Thus we see, through the insight of de Beauvoir, that women's bondage is women's confinement within the names imposed upon us by patriarchy--names that confine us according to our biological destiny and our relationships to men (and their children)--names that subordinate women and brand us as less than men. And, if patriarchy would bind women to what de Beauvoir calls our immanence--the givenness of Woman's role in patriarchal society largely determined by our biological function in service of the species and our relationships to others--then, she argues, liberation lies in our transcendence--in our ability to escape the confines of the immanence that patriarchy would enforce upon us. Liberation is the act of naming/defining ourselves.

De Beauvoir's insights into the nature of women's bondage and liberation reflect the language of existentialism--a language that is not as comfortable to feminists today. She speaks of immanence and transcendence almost as opposites, where transcendence is a "rising above" the givenness of one's situation to a subjectivity that "transcends" destiny. It is through transcendence that women can escape our bondage to an immanence that limits us to our biological destiny and to a relationality that keeps us named by others. Current

3

feminist thought, while affirming de Beauvoir's insights into the nature of women's bondage and liberation, seeks to affirm that liberation need not deny all aspects of what de Beauvoir has called immanence. Catherine Keller writes: "Is there some way to receive back into a newly empowered sense of self certain of those values she [de Beauvoir] discards as "immanent" without diluting the strength of freedom, individuality and transcendence she has advocated with such inspiring influence within the feminist trajectory?"[10] Keller is clearly searching for a way in which women can experience liberation and thus "new selfhood" while holding onto a sense of biological feminity and human relationality. While affirming that liberation lies in women's transcendence, current feminist thought speaks of transcendence as the ability (creativity/freedom) to weave the tapestry of life in a new way. The seemingly perpendicular axes of transcendence and immanence become intertwining spirals when women, in a moment of space within the rush of reality, see "freedom" and "transcendence" as the ability to gather the immanent threads of life and weave them into a new reality.[11]

Furthermore, while appropriating the thrust of de Beauvoir's argument that being fully human means defining oneself and not being defined by another, recent feminist thinkers avoid the dichotomy of "defining oneself" versus "being defined by relationality" that is characteristic of de Beauvoir. De Beauvoir tends to juxtapose "defining oneself" with "being defined by one's relationship to another" and thus characterizes a woman's self-definition as defining herself "in herself." Thus, real "humanity" begins with the autonomy to define oneself within oneself, i.e., apart from all human relationship. More recent feminist thinkers, while affirming that autonomy--the freedom to name oneself--is central to women's liberation, would see such a definition of selfhood as an abstraction. Contemporary feminist thought emphasizes that full human freedom--the freedom to define oneself--is always within the context of relationality. Thus one becomes fully human when naming oneself not "in oneself" but from within oneself, for as Robin Morgan suggests, freedom is "in the connections"[12] which means freedom is in-spite-of, or in-the-midst-of, or grounded-in--connections. The freedom she describes is not a woman's freedom to define herself "in

4

herself," but the freedom to create herself out of--or in the midst of--all of her connections.[13] Freedom means not being defined by connections or relationships. Freedom means the agency to name oneself within those relationships. The feminist understanding that freedom is grounded in connection and relationality does not, however, undercut the thrust of de Beauvoir's assertion and primary intuition that women's liberation means women's empowerment to define ourselves. Whereas, as Woman, women are defined from without, we can conclude that when women speak of liberation we mean the freedom _from_ being named from without according to biological functioning and/or relationality and the freedom to define ourselves from within, from our own center of being, within the context of our biological givenness and relationality.

Building on the insights of de Beauvoir, feminist philosopher Mary Daly has further traced the locus of women's bondage to patriarchy deep within women ourselves. Noting that the bondage of women to patriarchal systems has meant more than being defined and named from without and constrained within the confining roles of sexual stereotypes, Daly argues that women's bondage is internal as well--for the patriarchal facade has penetrated within. The names imposed upon women have been lodged within women's very being, constricting within us the human desire to be ones who define and name ourselves. Women have been invaded by a foreign identity, an identity that divides us within ourselves, cutting us off from our true human freedom. This "internalized patriarchal presence . . . carries with it feelings of guilt, inferiority, and self-hatred that extends itself to other women."[14] Instead of naming ourselves and claiming our own creative power, women begin to believe that the patriarchal names are true, that the foreign presence is our own, that our given names are our own. We begin to believe that we truly are subordinate, inferior, and even evil. Thus the foreign presence leads women to hate ourselves and other women as well. It divides women--cutting us off from without, from solidarity with other women, and from within, from our own integrity. Defined by patriarchy and taught to distrust our own intuitions, women are thus alienated from ourselves; we are denied any center from which to name ourselves and the world. We become dis-integrated. As Daly says:

5

Having been divided against the self, women want to speak, but remain silent. The desire for action is by and large reduced to acting vicariously through men. Instead of living out the dynamics of the authentic self, women generally are submerged in roles believed to be pleasing to males.[15]

And, unfortunately, the bondage spirals further. Denied ability to shape and name our own being, women are subject to the choices made for us and the names given to us. This means that from childhood women learn to appeal to and to please others. As Judith Plaskow has characterized de Beauvoir's argument:

Pleasing their fathers, lovers, husbands, defining themselves through them and through their children become ways of achieving justification at different stages of women's lives. Trained from childhood in the art of enchanting others, charming a man becomes the goal of a woman's existence. Marriage is her fate written in the heavens from the time she is twelve. From puberty, the life of the young girl becomes a period of waiting for The Man who will be her destiny.[16]

In needing to please others women are led into conflict with our deeper need to please and name ourselves. As de Beauvoir says, "In woman . . . there is from the beginning a conflict between her autonomous existence and her objective self, her 'being-the-Other': she is taught that to please she must try to please, she must make herself object; she should therefore renounce her autonomy."[17] Thus, not only is she "treated like a live doll and is refused liberty,"[18] but she herself "renounces her own autonomy" choosing to please others rather than choosing to name herself. "Thus a vicious circle is formed; for the less she exercises her freedom to understand, to grasp and discover the world about her, the less resources will she find within herself, the less will she dare to affirm herself as subject."[19] In her act of not only wearing the name that society would give her but grooming herself for it as well, a woman compromises her freedom to name herself. Running in a vicious circle at the periphery of her being, she denies her own freedom to

6

name herself from her own center of being and chooses instead to be named and created from without.

The freedom to name herself is not only a freedom, it is also a risk. To name herself, to define herself, to choose for herself, is to risk the possibility of failure, poor choice, mistake. For women, who in naming ourselves must first throw off, in a defiant act of exorcism, the names that society has thrust on us, this is especially risky. In naming ourselves women challenge the dominant society. This society has not taken the challenge lightly. In fact it seeks to persecute and label those who deviate from the "norm" as crazy or bad. And there is also the risk of disorientation as women pursue paths that are as yet unchartered, names as yet unspoken. Choosing to please others rather than risking the freedom to name ourselves thus appears to be a safer option for women. But, in choosing the "safe option," women run the risk of not exercising our freedom, and, worse yet, we risk losing the very freedom to "dare to affirm" ourselves as subjects.

It is possible to argue that since a woman "chooses" to be named, she still chooses from her own center of agency. However, this process of "choosing" must be seen in the context of a patriarchal society that rewards young girls from a very early age for pleasing others--living up to others' expectations--and thus living according to the choice of others and not from their own centers. If we take seriously de Beauvoir's warning of the vicious circle that depletes a young woman of her own freedom, then "choosing" to please others is less a result of decision and choice and more a euphemism for ingrained, reinforced, self-defeating behavior.[20]

Thus we see that women are in bondage to patriarchy through the imposition of names and definitions upon us. But, as Judith Plaskow argues, insofar as we accept those names and the safety and "status" that are offered by patriarchy along with them--accept them for the "rewards and welcome relief from the burden of freedom" they bring--women "are guilty of complicity in their own oppression."[21] This complicity in our own oppression, this evasion of freedom that eventually risks the loss of a woman's freedom to name herself, is, Plaskow suggests, women's sin.[22] De Beauvoir describes this

7

phenomenon as follows:

> To decline to be the Other, to refuse to be
> a party to the deal--this would be for
> women to renounce all the advantages
> conferred upon them by their alliance with
> the superior caste. Man-the-sovereign will
> provide woman-the-liege with material
> protection and will undertake the moral
> justification of her existence; thus she
> can evade at once both the economic risk
> and the metaphysical risk of liberty in
> which ends and aims must be contrived
> without assistance. Indeed, along with the
> ethical urge of each individual to affirm
> his existence, there is also the temptation
> to forgo liberty and become a thing. This
> is an inauspicious road, for he who takes
> it--passive, lost, ruined--becomes
> henceforth the creature of another's will,
> frustrated in his transcendence and
> deprived of every value. But it is an easy
> road; on it one avoids the strain involved
> in undertaking an authentic existence.
> When man makes of woman the Other, he may,
> then, expect her to manifest deep-seated
> tendencies toward complicity. Thus, woman
> may fail to lay claim to the status of
> subject because she lacks definite
> resources, because she feels the necessary
> bond that ties her to man regardless of
> reciprocity, and because she is often very
> well pleased with her role as the Other.[23]

Thus, women participate in our own bondage by
escaping from our freedom to name ourselves and
hiding in our status as objects. We "forgo our
liberty and become a thing." As Valerie Saiving has
described women's sin, it is suggested by such terms
as "triviality, distractibility, and diffuseness; [it
is the] lack of an organizing center or focus;
dependence on others for one's self-definition;
tolerance at the expense of standards of excellence;
. . . in short, under-development or negation of the
self."[24]

The sin of women, of participating in our own
bondage by choosing the comfort of another's name and
the less-than-human status of object/Other rather
than risk the freedom to name ourselves, I have

8

elsewhere called the sin of hiding.[25] It can be recognized in an essay written by a college freshwoman who, when asked to write a composition entitled, "Who Am I?" wrote the following:

> As I sit in my dorm room, the only thing I can think of is becoming Mrs. Peter Johnson. I can picture a small apartment which contains a flowered couch with matching chair, a small black and white T.V., and green carpeting through the house. I see myself in a pair of lounging pajamas with a little white apron on, so as not to get dirty. In the oven is a small beef roast with sliced carrots on the sides. The table is set for two with my plain brown Melmac dishes. The coffee is perking as I wait for Peter to come home from work. . . . I'm unhappy away from Peter, and until the day I become his wife, I am no one.[26]

At the time of the writing of this essay, her teacher notes, there was as yet no Peter Johnson in her life. Who he is does not seem to matter. He is not present, yet it is he who shall define who she is. She can foresee all the little details, the colors of the upholstery, the sliced carrots for dinner. Yet, until she is Mrs. Peter Johnson, she is no one. The sin of hiding is that she chooses to be named from without, by someone else, rather than name herself from within herself. She chooses to hide from her freedom to name herself. She is a college freshwoman, studying for a degree. She has talents and abilities that she could use to identify herself. She rejects the right to name herself, waiting for a man who shall define himself and in so doing, name her Mrs. Whoever-he-is. She puts herself on hold. She is, of course, choosing to name herself Mrs. Peter Johnson. But the point of the sin of hiding is not the total refusal to choose, it is choosing to allow herself to be named by another person and to live to please that other. It is the choice to be passive. It is the choice to live totally through another person because she has chosen not to be someone from within herself--from her own center of being. But note, to call this phenomenon the _sin_ of hiding, the sin of refusing to be someone within oneself, is not meant to suggest that one can be a "self" _without_ relationality. The sin of hiding

9

is when one chooses to be exclusively determined by relationships rather than defining oneself <u>within the context</u> of those relationships.

To charge women with complicity in our own bondage is to run the risk of "blaming the victim," of blaming women for our own bondage. This is not the intent of exploring the depth of women's complicity in our bondage. The temptation for women to sin is greatly reinforced by a society that has already reduced our options for naming ourselves, already given us a "safe" haven of sorts within the security of a named confinement, and already cut us off both from ourselves and from each other--thus severing the very bonds that might well provide the support that would enable us to take the risk of refusing complicity in our own confinement. As Mary Daly suggests: "When I write of women's complicity I mean a complicity that has in large measure been enforced by conditioning."[27]

Women's complicity in our own bondage through the sin of hiding, the sin of being named exclusively by relationships rather than naming ourselves from within ourselves in the context of relationships, is further complicated by the fact that women experience ourselves fundamentally as relational beings. Nancy Chodorow in <u>The Reproduction of Mothering</u> has shown that because <u>girls are mothered by women</u> they "come to experience themselves as less separate than boys, as having more permeable ego boundaries. Girls come to define themselves more in relation to others."[28] Thus, while experiencing herself as differentiated from her mother, a girl also <u>identifies with</u> her mother and feels deeply related to her. This identity in relationship with her mother, Chodorow argues, establishes for a girl a permeable or relational pattern of being a "self" in relation to other persons. The feminine oedipal complex, Chodorow notes for example, is not "simply a transfer of affection from mother to father and a giving up of mother,"[29] it is not a simple severing of relationship. Rather, "psychoanalytic research demonstrates the continued importance of a girl's external and internal relation to her mother, and the way her relation to her father is <u>added to</u> this."[30] (emphasis mine) Girls experience a continuity with their mothers that spirals out to include relationships with others. This continuity, according to Chodorow, is also due to the fact that

10

mothers tend to "experience their daughters as more like, and continuous with, themselves."[31] Thus girls emerge from the oedipal period "with a basis for 'empathy' built into their primary definition of self in a way that boys do not. Girls emerge with a stronger basis for experiencing another's needs or feelings as one's own."[32] Chodorow notes:

> From the retention of preoedipal attachments to their mother, growing girls come to define and experience themselves as continuous with others; their experience of self contains more flexible or permeable ego boundaries. . . . The basic feminine sense of self is connected to the world. . . .[33]

Thus she concludes, "feminine personality," described as it develops in a patriarchal culture where only women mother, "comes to include a fundamental definition of self in relationship."[34]

Feminists are beginning to argue that to understand oneself as a self in relationship is a strong point of women's experience.[35] To experience oneself as continuous with others is to be concerned for the care of the threads of continuity that weave people together. It is to recognize the mutual interdependence of all of creation and to have as one's central concern the preservation of all of that creation. Thus feminists are arguing that the experience of continuity between persons and between persons and creation is a crucial experience in the weaving together of a society in which each person has the opportunity to develop to her/his fullness.

But experiencing oneself fundamentally as relational--as continuous with another--is also to know a special difficulty in ever becoming a self who names herself from within--from her own center of being. On the one hand, women's experience of relationships to others as a fundamental part of ourselves often means we have difficulty in sorting out and finding our own centers in the midst of that relationality. On the other hand, the act of naming ourselves from within our own selves is perceived as a threat to our very real sense of continuity with those with whom we are in relationship (see chapter 3 for a further development of this point). It threatens to wrench us not only from "safety" and "status" within relationships but also from the very

11

relationships that have been central to our experience of who we are. Thus women's experience of ourselves as relational, as continuous with an other or others--and the centrality of that relationality to our sense of who we are, entails a certain temptation--the temptation of failing to differentiate ourselves _from_ that other, and a certain risk--the risk of failing to develop for ourselves a center of agency. As Chodorow explains, women who experience failure to differentiate themselves from another describe it as an experience of being empty of themselves and "women who feel empty of themselves feel that they are not being accorded a separate reality nor the agency to interpret the world in their own way."[36] Conversely, Anne Wilson Schaef, who refers to this experience of emptiness as an experience of an inner cavern, notes that the cavern "begins to get smaller" when "we begin to determine who we are from inside. . . ."[37] The experience of being continuous with others thus creates for a woman the risk of losing or never developing the "agency to interpret the world" in her own way--of losing the freedom to define and name herself from inside. She runs the risk of becoming what Elisabeth Moltmann-Wendel calls a "superadapted" woman--one who is so permeable and fluid that she has no sense of who she is from within herself. As Moltmann-Wendel notes:

> The self of a woman in our culture is a self without self-consciousness, without its own space. It is a flexible and constantly readapting self, almost never put to the test of deciding for itself. . . .
> This "super-adapted" woman . . . is the woman without a self of her own, not yet conscious of her own capabilities, her own lifestyle, or her own needs.[38]

Women's liberation is women's refusal to remain empty of ourselves. Such liberation does not necessarily mean wrenching ourselves from the web of relationality that constitutes our reality. The freedom to name herself means rather the freedom for a woman to reconstitute[39] relationships. However, where these relationships have been destructive ones for women, liberation may in fact mean the severing of some relationships. Women's liberation is a call for women to confess our sin, the sin, as Plaskow defines it, of the "failure to center the self, the

failure to take responsibility for one's own
life."[40] It is the call to refuse to center so
completely on our continuity to others, and on
maintaining that continuity by pleasing others, that
women become emptied of ourselves and forget that to
be human, to be free, is to have a center of agency
from which to interpret the world, from which to name
ourselves, from which to take responsibility for our
own lives.

If women are liberated through our refusal to
wear the patriarchal names given us--and our
insistence upon claiming our own center of agency
from which to participate in the naming of the world,
then women's bondage to patriarchal systems is
further compounded by the teachings of patriarchal
religions that have thwarted women's liberation by
identifing women's subordination and bondage as part
of the divine plan. "Man," de Beauvoir writes
"enjoys the great advantage of having a God endorse
the codes he writes."[41] Moreover, the patriarchal
system is bolstered by the very maleness of the deity
it worships. "If God is male," Mary Daly charges,
"then the male is God."[42] And if the male is God,
then women are subordinate--meant to be dominated.
Daly argues:

> The symbol of the Father God . . . has . . .
> rendered service to this type of society by
> making its mechanisms for the oppression of
> women appear right and fitting. If God in
> "his" heaven is a father ruling "his"
> people, then it is in the "nature" of
> things and according to divine plan and the
> order of the universe that society be
> male-dominated.[43]

Thus, the male-father-God reinforces not only the
superiority and god-likeness of the man, but it also,
inasmuch as the father God is one who rules and has
power over "his" people, reinforces the structures of
oppression built upon rulership and power over those
seen to be lower down in the hierarchy. Daly argues,
"within this context a mystification of roles takes
place: the husband dominating his wife represents
God 'himself.'"[44] Moreover, the persistent
maleness of God reifies divinity into a finite static
form. Thus, a male God not only verifies the
maleness of the patriarchal structure, but also
denies the divine any dynamic transcendence over

13

these structures and the ways human beings are in that structure. Reality itself is thought of as reified and unchanging. When God and the way "he" works is identified with the way the world is, then any notion of change and growth, Daly argues, is assumed to run counter to the divine intention. The feminist revolution, grounded in the intuition that subordination is not a full expression of women's humanity and that the way things are is not the way things have to be, is experienced then as a challenge to the patriarchal divinity "himself." Truly women who claim their transcendence over a patriarchal culture move, as Daly claims, "beyond god the father." However, as Daly herself grounds this move "beyond god the father" in the call of God the Verb,[45] women's liberation--at least in Daly's experience--is not the move beyond God, but the move beyond the patriarchal divinity.

Not only do religions centered on the worship of a male God legitimate the political and social order--granting authority to "fathers and sons in the institutions of society"[46] and delegitimizing any attempt to alter this order, they also, as Carol P. Christ argues, "create 'moods' and 'motivations' that keep women in a state of psychological dependence on men and male authority. . . ."[47] Patriarchal religions thus teach women to trust in an external, "superior," male authority, reinforcing patterns of dependency, of waiting and passivity, and keep women in a state of eternal childhood.[48] Thus, Christ continues, "religious symbol systems focused around exclusively male images of divinity create the impression that female power can never be fully legitimate or wholly beneficent."[49] A woman, then, "can never have the experience that is freely available to every man and boy in her culture, of having her full sexual identity affirmed as being in the image and likeness of God."[50] This leads, Christ argues, to a "mood" of "trust in male power as salvific and distrust of female power in herself and other women as inferior or dangerous."[51] Thus, a woman's need to be liberated by claiming her own authority is seriously thwarted.

Some contemporary patriarchal theologies, which reflect at least some awareness that the positions women are assigned amount to subordination within the ordained system and that our full humanity is thus qualified, still often reinforce women's bondage to patriarchal systems through what de Beauvoir calls an "instrument of deception."[52] Woman, she says "is asked in the name of God not so much to accept her inferiority as to believe that, thanks to Him, she is the equal of the lordly male."[53] In the realm of transcendence women are told that we are subordinate but equal.[54] Or, as Rosemary Radford Ruether identifies a different twist to the deception, women are told that our status is really one of superiority, and we are put on a pedestal and told not to change the situation.[55] This deceptive "equality" or "superiority" offered women by patriarchal theologies confuses women's perception of the very real inequality and subordination that exists and encourages a detachment from concern about systems of subordination and oppression.

Whereas some feminists, such as de Beauvoir, would argue that all religions are instruments of deception, and thus offer women no liberation but confusion and subordination, Mary Daly and others within the current movement of women's spirituality, argue that religious experience in itself (although by religious experience they refer to something different than that known in patriarchal religions) is central to women's experience of liberation. Part of the problem with religion for de Beauvoir is that it has tended to remove the locus of transcendence to a realm beyond this one and thus has not enhanced human transcendence as she understands it, the freedom to define and create and change this world. The whole thrust of the women's spirituality movement as I understand it, however, is that the nature of women's liberation--the experience of transcendence-- is a religious, spiritual experience--an experience that understands the realm of transcendence to be not the "other world" but this very world itself. To overcome the tension between these perspectives, I would argue that there are actually two notions of transcendence at work in this disagreement--one which means the ability to transcend, to create one's own response from one's own center, the other referring both to a realm detached from the present one and to the ability to so detach oneself and live "above" it all. Given the confusion that can follow from such a dual meaning for the term transcendence, perhaps Nelle Morton's suggestion that the word "transcending" better captures the meaning feminists are imputing to the word transcendence is helpful.[56] Whereas transcendence can point to an act within this world or to a locus beyond, the word transcending focuses on the act itself, and understands it to be an event that happens continually within the world as one participates in creating it. This is de Beauvoir's point--and is the experience women in feminist spirituality identify as religious or spiritual. The movement of women's spirituality then can be characterized as one that affirms that women's liberation is both an act of transcending that is a spiritual experience--and an experience that does not connote a luring-away-from the present reality.

Not only have patriarchal religions thwarted women's liberation by deceiving us through placing the locus of hope in a transcendent reality that is elsewhere, they have further perpetuated women's bondage to patriarchy in their specific teachings that women are the cause of evil. Specifically within the Christian tradition, Mary Daly charges, women have been bound through the myth of Eve, told in the second creation story found in Genesis 2, and through the extension of Eve's act of disobedience to include women in general as the source of all evil. Through Eve, she notes, evil was said to have entered the world. This assertion we can hear in the words of the early church father Tertullian: "<u>You</u> [woman] are the Devil's gateway. <u>You</u> are the unsealer of that forbidden tree. <u>You</u> are the first deserter of the divine Law. <u>You</u> are she who persuaded him whom the Devil was not valiant enough to attack. . . . On account of <u>your</u> desert, that is death, even the Son of God had to die."[57] The myth of Eve, her temptation and fall, Daly argues, "has projected a malignant image of the male-female relationship and of the 'nature' of women that is still deeply embedded in the modern psyche."[58] Naming Eve as the culpable one for the fall of humanity, Daly argues, "amounts to a cosmic false naming. It misnames the mystery of evil, casting it into the distorted mold of the myth of feminine evil."[59] It allows patriarchy to project guilt for the world's evil upon women and our sexuality and thus reinforces its prejudice against women.

This misnaming of women as Eve, the evil one, has reinforced systems that keep women in subordination, enhancing the domination of the superior caste. It has also reinforced the dividedness within women. Taught that we are the source of evil, women internalize this blame and

guilt in cycles of self-hatred, of mistrust of our
bodies, and of hatred of women in general. As
Elisabeth Moltmann-Wendel has said, when women
inspect Christian tradition:

> We find that the tradition from which we
> are supposed to live is full to the brim of
> hostility toward women. . . . the life
> assigned to women is not a whole life.
> According to one biblical passage, we women
> are to be saved by childbearing. . . . We
> are the first to sin. . . . In the
> distorted, patriarchal view our bodies have
> for far too long been considered
> embarrassing, unclean, repulsive.[60]

As Sheila Collins notes, told that we are to be saved
by obedience to the divinely ordained patriarchal
system by fulfilling our subordinate role, "many
women have internalized the myth of Eve's
disobedience so deeply that they are continually
plagued by excessive guilt whenever they feel the
desire to do something for themselves--to go beyond
or renege on their prescribed role as mother, wife,
or servant."[61]

Moreover, Mary Daly argues, Christianity further
enhances women's bondage because the Christian
savior, Jesus, cannot save women from our bondage.
On the one hand, as the male son of a male God, Jesus
has been used to reinforce the male system. (And, as
the second person of the male trinity, he has
undergirded the male "structure of existence.") It
is the male Jesus who is understood to be the son,
the image of God. Women as women could not possibly
bear such an image.[62] By our very womanliness, we
are excluded. On the other hand, Daly argues, Jesus
does not call women to claim our own powers and name
ourselves. Rather, as "savior" Jesus reinforces
women's dependence on a male--on an external
authority who by definition cannot save us--to save
us. Moreover, the Jesus willingly nailed to the
cross, does not work to save women but inspires us to
a "passive acceptance of suffering humility,
meekness, etc."[63]

Furthermore, the Christian religion amplifies
women's bondage when it teaches that pride and
self-centeredness are sin. Judith Plaskow notes,
"theology, insofar as it focuses on the sin of pride,

17

not only neglects women's experience, but adds to the pressures that keep women from being 'women and persons' by suggesting that self-assertion and the struggle for self-definition are sins."[64] Reinhold Niebuhr, whose <u>Nature and Destiny of Man</u> has been formative for theologians in this century in America, is an example of a Christian theologian for whom pride and self-centeredness are the chief form of human sin. He has been the focus of attack by several feminists for such a view.[65] We shall refer to Niebuhr's work to further explore how such a teaching on the nature of human sin promotes women's bondage to patriarchy.

Human beings, Niebuhr argues, are both finite and free. As finite, they are subject to a natural destiny--just as any other part of nature. But as free, they are able to transcend "mere" destiny and participate in shaping their own future. Living in the tension between finitude and freedom, Niebuhr argues, humanity's true nature lies in the law of love. Human persons cannot live merely for themselves, he says. Their transcendence/freedom ultimately leads them beyond themselves to live in loving relation with others.[66] The human problem as Niebuhr describes it is that instead of living by the law of love, humanity "comprehends the world and human relations from itself as the center."[67] The human self, Niebuhr argues, turns in on itself in a "vicious circle"[68] becoming self-centered, rather than extending itself outward in love. This vicious circle becomes a barrier between the individual and others, a barrier that creates a fortress from which the person fails to treat others lovingly as other subjects but treats them instead as objects over which it seeks to have power. This self-centered self, Niebuhr argues, is the human problem, and "in this state of preoccupation with itself must be 'broken' and 'shattered' or, in the Pauline phrase, 'crucified.'"[69] Once the old self-centered self is shattered in this experience, which Niebuhr calls conversion, a new self can be born, a new self that "is truly a real self because the vicious circle of self-centeredness has been broken. The self lives in and for others, in the general orientation of loyalty to and love of God."[70] Shattered in its pride and self-centeredness, the self as Niebuhr describes it can live a Christian existence in loving relation with others.

When the human problem is described as the sin of pride as it is in the theology of Reinhold Niebuhr, then pride and self-centeredness stand in the way of human fulfillment, which he says is expressed in the law of love--the law that human persons are ultimately relational beings living beyond the narrow confines of a limited self-centeredness. Yet we have seen earlier that women's sin is the sin of hiding and not the sin of pride. Women experience ourselves not as a walled fortress but as permeable selves with a natural empathy--a natural relatedness. Women's temptation, thus, is not to be self-centered as Niebuhr describes the "human situation," but to lose our center of being.[71] Thus, inasmuch as Christian theology identifies pride and self-centeredness as the sin of humanity, it calls women to confess the wrong sin. And, by identifying pride and self-centeredness as sin, it discourages women from finding our centers and taking pride in who we can be. Such a theology thus encourages women's bondage. As Plaskow argues, "the 'sin' which the feminine role in modern society creates and encourages in women is not illegitimate self-centeredness but failure to center the self, the failure to take responsibility for one's own life."[72] Thus, she says, "it is meaningless to say that this self can become a self [as Niebhur suggests] only through being shattered and turned to others, for its sin is precisely that it has no self to shatter."[73] Moreover, a woman's sin of hiding, of fearing to create a center from which to name and define herself and the world, is reinforced by a theology that identifies what she actually should be called to do--affirm her full humanity, become a centered self, and have a sense of pride in that--as sinful. Women are thus encouraged to hide. And those women who might realize the need to find our own centers and speak in our own voices are discouraged in the name of "sin" and are confronted by a father god who judges not only human pretensions, but the very centeredness that empowers women to name and define the world. Confronted with such a judgment, women who would seek our own self-center bear the weight of guilt for our "sin"--a guilt that further reinforces the guilt and self-hatred women feel for what Anne Wilson Schaef has called our "Original Sin of Being Born Female."[74] Whereas pride and self-centeredness may be a human problem from the perspective of Reinhold Niebuhr, Rosemary Ruether suggests that from women's

19

perspective pride, self-centeredness and the anger that can empower them are not problems but virtues. Where patriarchy has given women names and creates in us a false consciousness of who we are and what reality should be, Ruether argues that "anger corresponds to the power to transcend false consciousness and break its chains."[75] And "pride corresponds to the exorcism of demeaning self-images and the re-establishment of authentic personhood as the ground of one's being."[76] Anger and pride, as Ruether argues, are part of the liberating process whereby women find our own centers from which to name ourselves.

We have explored thus far in this chapter the nature of women's bondage and the factors that perpetuate it. Liberation, we have seen, is the shattering of that bondage and the false and constricting names it imposes on women, and it is the claiming of the freedom for women to name ourselves. It is, as Elisabeth Moltmann-Wendel says, when a woman says "a 'yes' to herself, with an attempt to accept herself with her own desires, joys, and fears. . . ."[77] It is when women strike out in spite of the guilt, self-hatred, sexual stereotypes, that have bound us, and declare, each in her own voice, "I am."[78] It is, Mary Daly says, a journey that involves the "exorcism of the internalized God-father in his various manifestations (his name is legion)."[79] It is the refusal to bear the names that have been thrust upon women. It is the process of dislodging from inside the false identity that has led women to be divided from ourselves. It is the discovery of a center of being and the beginning of a new integrity.

And how does this process--this journey toward liberation--begin? The journey for liberation begins, Mary Daly says, with the "realization that there is an existential conflict between the self and structures that have given such crippling security."[80] It begins, Rosemary Ruether suggests, "as an inner psychic revolution that gives her the transcending power to disaffiliate herself from male objectifications and to make her exodus from incorporations of her as an extension of male demands and alienation."[81] A woman's journey toward liberation begins with the realization that she is crippled--meaning both that she is crippled, divided within, without the wholeness to function as a complete human being and that she is being crippled, bound, deformed, constrained. It begins with the realization that her crippled state has offered a security that will be risked in the journey toward liberation.

But the journey begins with the even prior realization, if we examine Daly's assertion, that she is in conflict with the state of "crippling security." That is, the journey begins with an awareness that there is another possibility than the one in which she finds her crippling security. This awareness happens, Daly suggests, when "the old simple meanings, role definitions, and life expectations" are realized as "crippling" and are "rooted out and rejected openly."[82]

In a very real sense, then, the process of liberation as experienced by women is a process of self-liberation and self-awareness. The awareness of bondage, Daly has revealed, is a woman's own. As Ruether suggests, it is an "inner psychic revolution"--a turning and churning inside that, I would suggest, reflects a change in a woman's center of being. Whereas patriarchal bondage means for women that we are named from without and begin indeed to see ourselves as reflected in the eyes of patriarchy, the process of liberation is one in which a woman comes to awareness. That is, she sees with her own eyes, from her own center of being. This is the nature of the "inner psychic revolution" Ruether speaks of. Women no longer perceive reality through the eyes of patriarchy. We see from within, from our own center of being. We are suddenly aware of "crippling security." We suddenly realize a new possibility. This awareness reflects a discovery of a new center within, a center from which a woman is then able to recognize her oppression, name it as such, turn to confront a world without models, and create herself in spite of it.

Although this process of liberation is one each woman must go through for herself since her awareness is her own, the process is also a dialogue. Paulo Freire suggests in his Pedagogy of the Oppressed that the process of liberation from oppression is the process of conscientizacion--a process of coming to awareness of one's own oppression and beginning to take action to overcome that oppression.[83] No one, Freire argues, "can be liberated by others."[84]

21

But, although no one can liberate another, he argues that the process of liberation can be encouraged by a "dialogue" in which the oppressed are encouraged to name their own bondage and begin to say their own word and name the world.[85] Thus the process of liberation is aided by a dialogue with others in which one can begin to speak and name and find one's own center of awareness.

For Daly, Ruether and others within the movement of women's spirituality, this experience of awareness and empowerment women have when we risk a life without models and dare to name ourselves is the experience of the divine, by whatever name the divine is recognized. Not all women would identify the experience in this way. Yet Sheila Collins argues:

> Although most women do not experience this revelation in ecclesiastical or religious terms, I believe that it has all the hallmarks of what we used to think of as religious revelation, although the impulse is felt to grow from within, to burgeon up and out rather than in the old terms, to break in upon the human person or community from without.[86]

She goes on to suggest: "Perhaps this is what divine incarnation means for today: that God is that force, that energizing and life-generating spirit which is present in the painful struggles of people for liberation and self-actualization."[87]

Mary Daly speaks about this revelatory experience in a two-fold fashion. On the one hand, she speaks of God the Verb, who "acts as a moral power summoning women and men to act out of [their] deepest hope and to become who [they] can be."[88] "This Verb--the Verb of Verbs--is intransitive. It need not be conceived as having an object that limits its dynamism."[89] This God the Verb stands in judgment of the patriarchal reified God the Noun who is static and verifies the static patriarchal system. This God is dynamic, unfolding, summoning people, men and women, to be who they can be. This God is not a Noun, nor does this God name. Rather, God the Verb calls people to realize their bondage, to discover their "power of speech"[90] and to name themselves. This God is beyond all names, for "in hearing and naming ourselves out of the depths, women

22

are naming toward God. . . ."[91] As Nelle Morton says,

> Fancy! A great ear at the heart of the universe--at the heart of our common life--hearing women to speech--to our own speech.[92]

In a reversal of traditional Christian affirmation, Daly suggests, "In the beginning was not the word. In the beginning is the hearing."[93] This is a God who calls persons to envision new possibilities beyond models and to name the old ones as false. This is a God who beckons people to speak in their own voices and name themselves, and whose listening presence draws them toward the dynamic unfolding which is the divine being.

But the source of all power/being, Daly reveals, is also experienced deep within.[94] Daly says, "women who are confronting the nothingness which emerges when one turns one's back upon the pseudo-reality offered by patriarchy are by that very act saying 'I am,' that is, confronting our own depth of being."[95] As women experience the "absence of the old Gods" we are "in a situation to experience presence. This is not the presence of a super-reified Something, but of a power of being which both is, and is not yet."[96] This power comes from "living in existential courage"--a courage that points to "our deep sources, our spring."[97] This "is a sense of power, not of the 'wholly other,' but of the Self's be-ing"[98]--a power that is both the woman's own and drawn from, and in response to, a deeper source. This experience of participation in power, "is strength giving, not in the sense of 'supernatural elevation' through 'grace' or of magic mutation through miracle drugs, but in the sense of creative unfolding of the Self."[99] This source bubbles up and fills the hollowness that is left in the absence of the false selves that the journey to liberation exorcises. To experience the source is to experience a fullness (and not an emptying or shattering) of being, a fullness that is the empowerment to speak one's own name. Thus Daly reveals that women's experience of liberation and empowerment is the revelation of the presence of the divine--both as beckoning from beyond and as empowering from within--both as God the Verb and the Goddess within.[100]

Whether or not all women would agree with Mary Daly that the experience of liberation points to an ontological source of human empowerment, there is a consensus that what women's liberation is about is the experience of empowerment--expressed in this chapter as the empowerment to name ourselves. But, although the language of divinity is not comfortable to all women, Carol P. Christ argues that the image of the Goddess within is one that women need. Just as the male God has validated male power and taught women to distrust ourselves and thus enhanced our bondage, so "the symbol of the Goddess" can empower women since it can be "the acknowledgment of the legitimacy of female power as a beneficent and independent power."[101] Women are taught by male symbols and male structures of authority to put our trust in an external authority. Women's liberation from male symbols and structures, Christ argues, leads us to an affirmation of our own independent power. No longer trusting in an external authority to give us our name, women are free to name ourselves from our own center of authority. The Goddess within, Christ argues, does not function for women as an idol, or as another external authority. Rather, she is the symbol for the authority, the empowerment, within each woman. She thus serves to encourage women to claim our own authority.

Moreover, Christ argues, the Goddess symbol is for women "the affirmation of the female body and the life cycle expressed in it."[102] Symbolized as Eve, the cause of evil, women have been charged, at least by a major strain of the Judeo-Christian tradition, with sexuality (as if sexuality is something to be "charged" with), and our bodies have been declared "unclean," in need of rituals of purification. Sexuality, projected onto women and denied in men, has been mistrusted as well. The Goddess, Christ argues, can symbolize for women not only our own authority but the reclaiming of our bodies and their processes as good and as an integral part of who we are. As Woman, women are consigned to be body--and are devalued for it. As liberated women, we are able to be more than "only body" while affirming that the body is good. Our bodies, then, no longer keep us in bondage to our biological destinies, but are the source of feelings and connections, a source of strength. As Elisabeth Moltmann-Wendel suggests, women's liberation means "that corporeality and physical experience are no longer suppressed but

24

accepted."103 This accepting of our bodies then would mean that "anatomy would not be fate any longer, it would be opportunity."104

As women in our sudden "psychic awareness" venture out into the non-being that is the world without patriarchal models, we journey deep within ourselves. There we discover our own voices, voices we have not been able to hear and recognize as our own before. Finding our own voices, we begin to speak. We emerge as "free persons whose lives communicate a kind of contagious freedom."105 This is the freedom to "spark" to speak "with tongues of fire" that ignite "the divine Spark in women."106 It is the freedom to speak from deep within our own center and to spark the contagious freedom in another--to create an environment in which another can come to her own psychic awareness and begin to reach deep within and find her own center of being and, as some would affirm, her own connection to the source of being, to the "Goddess within."

As women come to see our own brokenness and dividedness in the patriarchal system and risk the pain of giving birth to a new wholeness, so we reach out to name and heal the brokenness of the world. Daly says, "by living out our own promise, we are breaking the brokenness in human existence that has been effected by means of the constructs of alienation. . . . we are breaking the dam of sex stereotyping that stops the flow of being. . . ."107

As women's experience has revealed, patriarchy has broken women, divided us within and without. And as it has broken women, it has broken the rest of reality as well. As Jürgen Moltmann has said, patriarchy cuts men in half also, cutting them off from their human fullness, their connection to the source of all being. Thus, women's liberation means human liberation as well. As women spin deep within our own brokenness to discover the source of our being and discover the "lost thread of connectedness within the cosmos,"108 we can begin to weave the whole world in a new way.

Women experience our liberation as a call to selfhood, to self-affirmation--the call to give birth to ourselves, to name ourselves and to grow into our fullness. It is the process in which we become centered individuals, finding centers from which to define, create, decide, and integrate our experience and to refuse the "seductive summons of the Passive Voices. . . ."[109] It is the journey on which women begin, as Catherine Keller has suggested, to speak "as ones with authority."[110]

Women's liberation is as well the movement out of religions that deny us our full human freedom and teach us to distrust our own voices, our own authority. And Christianity, we have seen, has been named as one of the religions that has participated in reinforcing women's bondage to patriarchy.

We have seen in this chapter then that when women speak of liberation from patriarchy we mean our empowerment to speak in our own voices and name ourselves. In Chapter II, then, we shall begin to ask the question whether or not Christianity--in the light of the arguments in this chapter--can empower women's liberation. Can Christianity encourage women to be aware of and name our oppression? Can it empower women to name ourselves, to speak in our own voices?

NOTES

[1]For a study of these forms of bondage see "The Second Passage" in Mary Daly, Gyn/Ecology: The Metaethics of Radical Feminism (Boston: Beacon Press, 1978).

[2]Simone de Beauvoir, translated and edited by H. M. Parshley, The Second Sex (New York: Vintage Books/Random House, 1974), pp. xxxiii-xxxiv.

[3]Ibid., p. xviii.

[4]Ibid., p. 42.

[5]Ibid., p. xix.

[6]Ibid., p. xviii.

[7]Ibid., p. xix.

[8]Elisabeth Moltmann-Wendel and Jürgen Moltmann, "Becoming Human in New Community" in The Community of Women and Men in the Church, ed. Constance F. Parvey (Philadelphia: Fortress Press, 1983), p. 32.

[9]For a study of how this type of a split in the male has led to the denial of "nature" in man and been manifest in an overt way in pornography, rape, and the abuse of women, see Susan Griffin, Poronography and Silence: Culture's Revenge Against Nature (New York: Harper & Row, 1981).

[10]Catherine E. Keller, "From a Broken Web: Sexism, Separation, and Self" (Ph.D. dissertation, Claremont Graduate School, 1984), p. 51. Keller's dissertation has since been published under the title From a Broken Web: Separation, Sexism, and Self (Boston: Beacon Press, 1986).

[11]The intuition that life is interconnected and that freedom is experienced through the ties of "immanence" is one that pervades contemporary feminist writing. See for example: Mary Daly's Gyn/Ecology and Pure Lust; Elisabeth Dodson Gray's Green Paradise Lost; an anthology on feminism and nonviolence edited by Pam McAllister, Reweaving the Web of Life; Adrienne Rich's A Wild Patience Has Taken Me This Far; Rosemary Radford Ruether's New

27

Woman New Earth; Marjorie Suchocki's God, Christ, Church; and Alice Walker's The Color Purple. See also the psychological studies referred to in Chapter III of this work.

[12]Robin Morgan, The Anatomy of Freedom: Feminism, Physics, and Global Politics (Garden City, New York: Anchor Press/Doubleday, 1982), p. 38. Morgan's book explores the notion of freedom from the experience of women and insists that freedom is ultimately relational. "It lives in the connections." Catherine Keller's dissertation is a proposal for a feminist ontology drawing on similar intuitions. See also Caroline Whitbeck, "A Different Reality: Feminist Ontology" in Beyond Domination: New Perspectives on Women and Philosophy, ed. Carol C. Gould (Totowa, New Jersey: Roman & Allanheld, Publishers, 1984).

[13]Freedom that is the freedom to define oneself "in oneself" (cut off from all connections) is not freedom at all but a denial of real connections, interdependencies and dependencies. See Morgan's "The Handmaiden of the Holy Man" in Anatomy of Freedom for a mythical exploration of this intuition.

[14]Mary Daly, Beyond God the Father: Toward a Philosophy of Women's Liberation (Boston: Beacon Press, 1973), p. 50.

[15]Ibid., p. 48.

[16]Judith Plaskow, Sex, Sin and Grace: Women's Experience and the Theologies of Reinhold Niebuhr and Paul Tillich (Washington, D.C.: University Press of America, 1980), p. 32.

[17]de Beauvoir, p. 316.

[18]Ibid., p. 316.

[19]Ibid., p. 316.

[20]See Chapter III of this work for further discussion of how women who please others lose their center of agency and live in the eyes of others.

[21]Plaskow, pp. 64-65.

[22]Mary Daly also refers to women's "complicity" in our bondage to patriarchy. See Daly, Beyond God the Father, p. 49.

[23]de Beauvoir, pp. xxiv-xxv.

[24]Valerie Saiving, "The Human Situation: A Feminine View" in Womanspirit Rising: A Feminist Reader in Religion ed. by Carol P. Christ and Judith Plaskow (San Francisco: Harper & Row, 1979), p. 327. Originally published in Journal of Religion, 40 (April, 1960) by the University of Chicago Press; Copyright 1960 by the University of Chicago.

[25]Susan Dunfee, "The Sin of Hiding: A Feminist Critique of Reinhold Niebuhr's Account of the Sin of Pride," Soundings 65 (Fall 1982): 316-317. In the article I develop the sin of hiding from the schema developed by Reinhold Niebuhr. Since it is developed from his theory of human nature, the sin of hiding is a human (and not just women's) possibility. I refer to it as the sin of women because it is best revealed in the lives of women. Dan Rhoades has suggested (see class notes Spring 1980) however that the sin of hiding may well be the sin of our entire generation.

[26]Sarah Harder, "The Wife I Wasn't Meant To Be," Redbook Magazine, February, 1973, p. 40.

[27]Daly, Beyond God the Father, p. 49.

[28]Nancy Chodorow, The Reproduction of Mothering: Psychoanalysis and the Sociology of Gender (Berkeley, University of California Press, 1978), p. 93. This is a study of girls in a society where only women mother--a patriarchal society--and thus is an observation of how girls experience themselves in such a society. Chodorow's observations do not intend to be universal for all women. And, we should also note, she does not ground this different experience of women in biology.

[29]Ibid., p. 92.

[30]Ibid., p. 92-93. Caroline Whitbeck in "A Different Reality: Feminist Ontology" in Beyond Domination: New Perspectives on Women and Philosophy, Carol C. Gould, ed., (Totowa, NJ, Roman and Allanheld, 1984), charges Chodorow with using a

dualistic approach that "presuppose the masculist opposition of self and other" (p. 72). Where I would agree with Whitbeck that Chodorow does make use of material that does betray such a tendency, Chodorow uses the material to suggest that women's experience is one of connectedness. Thus although Chodorow may reflect the self/other dichotomy, her intuitions into the connectedness of women's reality have been used by other feminists, i.e., Catherine Keller, to ground an ontology of connectedness.

[31]Ibid., p. 166.

[32]Ibid., p. 167.

[33]Ibid., p. 169.

[34]Ibid., p. 169. For a study of how exclusive female mothering has reinforced sexual stereotypes and the accompanying "malaise" of the culture see Dorothy Dinnerstein, The Mermaid and the Mintour: Sexual Arrangements and Human Malaise (New York: Harper & Row, 1976).

[35]See Catherine Keller, From a Broken Web: Separation, Sexism, and Self, and Jean Baker Miller, Toward a New Psychology of Women (Boston: Beacon Press, 1976).

[36]Chodorow, p. 100.

[37]Anne Wilson Schaef, Women's Reality: An Emerging Female System in the White Male Society (Minneapolis: Winston Press, 1981), p. 34.

[38]Elisabeth Moltmann-Wendel, Liberty, Equality, Sisterhood: On the Emancipation of Women in Church and Society, trans. Ruth Gritsch (Philadelphia: Fortress Press, 1978), pp. 76-77.

[39]"I have to cast my lot with those
who age after age, perversely,
with no extraordinary power,
reconstitute the world."
Adreinne Rich, The Dream of a Common Language (New York: Norton, 1978), "Natural Resources" #14, p. 67.

[40]Plaskow, p. 92.

[41]de Beauvoir, p. 691.

[42]Daly, _Beyond God the Father_, p. 19.

[43]_Ibid._, p. 13.

[44]_Ibid._, p. 13.

[45]_Ibid._, p. 34.

[46]Carol P. Christ, "Why Women Need the Goddess: Phenomenological, Psychological, and Political Reflections" in _The Politics of Women's Spirituality: Essays on the Rise of Spiritual Power Within the Feminist Movement_, ed. Charlene Spretnak (Garden City, New York: Anchor Press/Doubleday, 1982), p. 73.

[47]_Ibid._, p. 73.

[48]See de Beauvoir's _The Second Sex_ (p. 692) for a discussion of women as the eternal children.

[49]Christ, p. 73.

[50]_Ibid._, p. 73.

[51]_Ibid._, p. 73.

[52]de Beauvoir, p. 691.

[53]_Ibid._, p. 691.

[54]See "The Triumph of Patriarchalism in the Theology of Karl Barth" in _Women and Religion: A Feminist Sourcebook of Christian Thought_ ed. Elisabeth Clark and Herbert Richardson (New York: Harper & Row, 1977).

[55]See "The Descent of Woman: Symbol and Social Condition" in Ruether's _New Woman New Earth: Sexist Ideologies and Human Liberation_ (New York: A Crossroad Book/The Seabury Press, 1975).

[56]Conversation with Nelle Morton, Claremont, California, May 31, 1984. See also Charlene Spretnak's "Introduction" to _The Politics of Women's Spirituality_ for a positive statement of women's spirituality as a source of women's power. See also p. 22 of this chapter.

[57]Quoted in _Religion and Sexism_ ed. Rosemary

Radford Ruether (New York: Simon and Schuster, 1974), p. 157.

[58]Daly, Beyond God the Father, p. 45.

[59]Daly, Beyond the Father, p. 47.

[60]Elisabeth Moltmann-Wendel and Jürgen Moltmann, "Becoming Human in New Community," p. 34.

[61]Sheila D. Collins, A Different Heaven and Earth: A Feminist Perspective on Religion (Valley Forge: Judson Press, 1974), p. 83.

[62]Daly, Beyond God the Father, p. 77.

[63]Ibid., p. 77--which leaves us with the paradoxical notion that women do not "identify" with Jesus as the Son of God but do identify with him as "sacrificial victim."

[64]Plaskow, p. 68.

[65]Besides Plaskow, Valerie Saiving and I have published articles critiquing Niebuhr. See notes 24 and 25 in this chapter for references.

[66]Although Niebuhr argues that self-sacrificial love is the highest form of the law of love, I have argued elsewhere that the self is not sacrificed in the act of love but is transformed into a real self that lives beyond the boundaries that humans in their sinfulness create. Thus, I interpret Niebuhr's law of love to point not to the sacrifice of self but to the relationality between selves open and permeable to one another. See Chapter IV for further development of this view.

[67]Reinhold Niebuhr, The Nature and Destiny of Man, vol. 2 (New York: Charles Scribner's Sons, 1943), p. 108.

[68]Ibid., p. 110.

[69]Ibid., p. 109.

[70]Ibid., p. 110.

[71]Women's experience of ourselves as permeable would seem to agree with Niebuhr's intuition that the

law of humanity is the law of love . . . that human beings should naturally lead lives connected to each other. However, whereas Niebuhr grounds his argument for the law of love in the experience of transcendence that lifts the self beyond itself, women experience the "law of love" through our initial connectedness-or what de Beauvoir might refer to as our immanence! The transcendent motion in women's experience as we have explored it in this chapter is not a move beyond self-centeredness as Niebuhr suggests, but the motion to centeredness. The difference in perception suggests that what may seem to be the solution to the human problem from Niebuhr's perspective is not a solution to women's problem but in fact makes the problem worse.

[72]Plaskow, p. 92.

[73]Ibid., p. 156.

[74]Schaef, p. 23.

[75]Rosemary Radford Ruether, "Sexism and the Theology of Liberation," The Christian Century, December 12, 1973, p. 1226. See also "The Power of Anger in the Work of Love: Christian Ethics for Women and Other Strangers," by Beverly Wildung Harrison, Union Seminary Quarterly Review 36 supplement (1981): 41-43, 54-57.

[76]Ruether, "Sexism and the Theology of Liberation," p. 1226.

[77]Moltmann-Wendel, Liberty, Equality, Sisterhood, p. 82.

[78]Daly, Beyond God the Father, p. 36.

[79]Daly, Gyn/Ecology, p. 1.

[80]Daly, Beyond God the Father, p. 24.

[81]Ruether, "Sexism and the Theology of Liberation," p. 1226.

[82]Daly, Beyond God the Father, p. 24.

[83]See Paulo Freire, Pedagogy of the Oppressed (New York: The Seabury Press, 1974).

84Ibid., p. 53.

85Ibid., p. 13. Peter Berger in Pyramids of Sacrifice (New York: Basic Books, 1974) charges Freire with an elitism where the pedagogue who leads others to their conscientizacion is the possessor of the awareness others need to claim. But, if the awareness of one's oppression is one's own, then one must discover and name it from one's own perspective. Thus, one must question whether or not there can be a "pedagogy" of the oppressed. I agree with Berger that there is a problem in Freire's model. The purpose of dialogue as I am suggesting it here however is not to lead another, but to listen and encourage another that in the process of being heard, the speaker will discover her own voice. The speaker thus is allowed her own journey--dialogue allows her to verbalize. The model of leading a woman to her consciousness of oppression has led some women to attack their sisters rather than hear them into speech and undercuts the very notion of having one's own voice and authority that is central to women's liberation.

86Collins, p. 191.

87Ibid., p. 191.

88Daly, Beyond God the Father, p. 32.

89Ibid., p. 34.

90Ibid., p. 10.

91Ibid., p. 33.

92Quoted in Mary Daly, Gyn/Ecology, p. 313.

93Ibid., p. 424.

94This experience of the divine deep within is reflected in Daly's Gyn/Ecology whereas God the Verb is central to her argument in Beyond God the Father. In the later book much of the summoning imagery of God the Verb has been lost. The movement becomes one that centers deeply inward as a woman begins to find her own center and spiral deep within herself. It would thus be possible to argue that only the second experience, as the most recent, is valid. I am assuming, however, that both experiences reflect

34

valid experiences on women's journey to liberation. God the Verb beckons women to name--and in naming, we experience within ourselves a power Daly says is the source of all Being.

[95]Daly, Beyond God the Father, p. 46.

[96]Ibid., p. 36.

[97]Daly, Gyn/Ecology, p. 21.

[98]Ibid., p. 49.

[99]Ibid., p. 49.

[100]Note: Daly refers to the Goddess as affirming "the life-loving be-ing of women and nature." Gyn/Ecology, p. xi.

[101]Christ, "Why Women Need the Goddess," p. 75. This paragraph is drawn from this article. For a similar approach to how women's liberation is a journey beyond patriarchal authorities to an internal authority symbolized in the Goddess, see Naomi Goldenberg, Changing of the Gods: Feminism and the End of Traditional Religions (Boston: Beacon Press, 1979).

[102]Christ, p. 77.

[103]Moltmann-Wendel, Liberty, Equality, Sisterhood, p. 66.

[104]Ibid., p. 66.

[105]Daly, Beyond God the Father, p. 10.

[106]Daly, Gyn/Ecology, p. 319.

[107]Daly, Beyond God the Father, p. 158.

[108]Daly, Gyn/Ecology, p. 390.

[109]Ibid., p. 318.

[110]Class discussion with C. Keller, School of Theology at Claremont, Claremont, California, Fall 1982.

CHAPTER II

Christianity: Necessarily Patriarchal?

We have seen in Chapter I that women's
liberation means women having the freedom to name
ourselves and to speak in our own voices. This
liberation is grounded in a woman's growing awareness
that the givenness of her womanhood--her "nature" as
defined by patriarchal society--is not in fact <u>given</u>
at all. It is, rather, a fabrication, a projection,
a confinement. The move toward liberation is the
move to name confinement and oppression as they
are--both in the society and as they are internalized
within each woman. Liberation is thus both an
exorcism and an exercise of freedom. It is the
naming of the demon and of the new possibility. It
is both an internal and an external motion as a woman
gives birth to herself while struggling to create a
new environment in which women and other oppressed
persons can be encouraged to name our confinement and
begin to name ourselves. It is both an act of
tearing away from the old and of creating a new space
where this new life can be experienced. And it is a
healing act as women begin from our new space to mend
the brokenness and alienation that patriarchal
society creates.

Patriarchal religions, we have noted in Chapter
I, do not liberate women. Rather, through their male
deities and pronouncements on the divine order of
creation, they affirm and reinforce patriarchal
patterns of oppression and confinement. At their
"best" they tell women we are equal but subordinate
to men--ordained to fulfill our biological destiny.
At their worst, they villify women--naming us the
cause of all evil, treating us as sub-human. Women
are not liberated through such teachings. Rather, we
learn to mistrust ourselves and each other--and to
distrust as well any intuitional awareness that
things should be different than they are. Women,
through patriarchal religions, are taught rather to
trust in males--in husbands, fathers, and patriarchal
gods. Our calling is to obedience, humility and
subservience.

In light of Chapter I, the question I propose to
begin to engage in this chapter is whether
Christianity can empower women's liberation. Despite
the fact that Christianity has throughout most of its

history been a patriarchal religion, can Christianity affirm women's growing awareness of the oppressive character of patriarchy and offer an environment in which women can be encouraged to name ourselves and speak in our own voices?

To propose such a question is to raise the prior question of whether Christianity is necessarily patriarchal. That is, as Jürgen and Elisabeth Moltmann have suggested, is it possible that Christianity has itself been in bondage to patriarchy?[1] This is a possibility that not all women are even willing to admit. Mary Daly, Carol P. Christ, and Naomi Goldenberg, among others, argue to the contrary that the maleness of Christianity is central to it.[2] These "revolutionaries," as classified by Christ and Judith Plaskow in the introduction to their anthology, Womanspirit Rising,[3] argue that women's spirituality must lead women beyond patriarchal religions ("beyond god the father") to a spirituality where women are affirmed as good and powerful and in the divine image.[4] The purpose of this chapter will be to ask, in the light of this criticism, whether Christianity is necessarily patriarchal. Can it offer to women a tradition that can be used against patriarchy?

Not all feminists agree with their "revolutionary" sisters that Christianity is patriarchal to its core. Phyllis Trible[5] in her structural Biblical work argues, for example, that one can see in the very structure of the text a liberating intention. Similarly, Letty Russell and Rosemary Radford Ruether,[6] in their liberation theologies (and these are only a sampling of scholars, male and female, who have argued that Christianity can call women to our liberation--to be "all we're meant to be"[7]) have affirmed that there is a "usable" or "liberating" kernel or core[8] of Christianity that can be reclaimed and used for the liberation of women despite Christianity's patriarchal history. Arguing that the prophetic movement in the Judeo-Christian tradition is one that has assailed all forms of idolatry and oppression and can be used against the patriarchal idolatry of present Christianity, Ruether (and Russell makes similar arguments) argues that Christianity can be a vital source for women's liberation.[9]

Although the Judeo-Christian tradition has

indeed tended to "ignore or directly sanction
sexism," Ruether argues that it is possible for
feminists to "transform" the "inheritance" of that
tradition into a tradition that can be liberating for
women.[10] She states, "All significant works of
culture have depth and power to the extent that they
have been doing something else besides just
sanctioning sexism."[11] Women, she says, "can
discover this critical element and apply it to
themselves."[12] In so doing women "will make it say
things it never said before."[13] For Ruether, the
"something else" that the Judeo-Christian religion
has been doing is the work of liberation. The
prophetic-messianic tradition of Christianity, she
argues, has been a liberating tradition and can be
transformed "to say things it never said before"--to
be engaged in the liberation of women.

This liberating tradition, Ruether says, can be
discovered in the Bible. She argues: "Unlike most
of Christian theology, the Bible, for the most part,
is not written from the standpoint of world power,
but from the standpoint of people who take the side
of the disadvantaged."[14] This perspective
"inclines the Bible to a view of God as One who comes
to vindicate the oppressed. God judges those who
'grind the faces of the poor, the widow and orphan';
God 'puts the mighty down from their thrones and
fills the poor with good things.'"[15] Basically,
she argues, this standpoint with the disadvantaged
"means that the God-language of the Bible tends to be
judgmental and destabilizing toward the existing
social order and its hierarchies of power; religious,
social and economic."[16] Whereas "much of world
religion has functioned ontocratically to provide a
'sacred canopy' by which the existing order is
stabilized,"[17] Ruether notes that the God of
Christianity, "the prophetic God who takes the side
of the poor, drowns the horsemen of Pharoah and leads
the slaves out of Egypt . . ."[18] is a God "who
undercuts the agenda of most of what has been
identified as 'religion.'"[19]

Ruether notes moreover that the Bible reveals
not an affirmation of existing social orders, but a
primary vision of an "alternative future," which is a
"new society of peace and justice that will arise
when the present systems of injustice have been
overthrown."[20] Although this vision becomes
apocalyptic "when Israel despairs of immediate hopes"

and in the New Testament "loses its base in social hope altogether and becomes 'other-worldly,'" Ruether argues that "its roots remain those of social criticism and the hope for an alternative society on this earth."[21]

Finally, Ruether says, the Bible contains "a remorseless critique of religion."[22] She notes, this critique "is directed at degeneration of religion into cult and rote, especially the use of religion to justify those already in power and to ignore God's agenda of social justice."[23] And the Synoptic Gospels "are framed as a continual confrontation between the iconoclastic messianic prophet and the scribal and priestly leaders. . . ."[24]

Thus, Ruether argues, Christianity offers to women a "critical pattern of prophetic thought"[25]--a pattern that reflects the perspective of the disadvantaged, that understands God as one who upsets unjust social orders, and that criticizes idolatrous religious systems that "ignore God's agenda of social justice." This "critical pattern," Ruether argues, is "the usable tradition for feminism in the Bible"[26]--a tradition women can claim and transform "to say things it never said before" to empower women's liberation from patriarchal religions and societies in which women are the disadvantaged, the victims of injustice.

But can this liberating tradition Ruether finds in the Bible be usable for women in our journey towards liberation? Can women claim this tradition to "say things it never said before" in the cause of women's liberation from patriarchy? Carol P. Christ, in an ongoing debate with Ruether, argues that one cannot simply cling to a "usable" part of Christian tradition and assume that it will be liberating without considering the patriarchal aspects of that tradition. Such a move, Christ suggests, "may not acknowledge the depth of the damage that ha[s] been done to female and male psyches by the symbol of God as male."[27] One cannot, she charges, appropriate a liberating intention or tradition without dealing with the fact that the God who is attested to in the prophetic movement is in fact a male deity. Moreover, Christ argues, since "many of the priestly writings are concerned with excluding women from the central roles in the cult" she "cannot agree with

Ruether's statement that 'the Bible for the most part
is not written from the standpoint of world
power.'"[28] Christ continues, the prophetic
tradition itself "certainly has contributed to the
antipathy toward female leadership and female
God/dess symbolism in Judaism and Christianity" since
"Goddess religions in which women play key roles were
among the religions condemned by the prophets. . .
."[29] Moreover, "the fact that the judgment on the
rich in favor of the poor in the prophetic tradition
is delivered by a male God" makes Christ "question
the validity of the 'critical and liberating'
potential of this tradition for women . . . [since]
one of the messages conveyed to women by this
tradition is that they must be judged, punished, and
forgiven by a male authority figure in order to be
saved."[30] Thus Christ questions whether, given the
inherent maleness of the Christian deity, one is
truly able to distill any liberating potential
without coming to grips with and addressing the
problem of maleness. Furthermore, she questions
whether Ruether can claim the liberating intent of
the prophetic movement for women when that very
movement has stood against those movements of women
in history from which Christ argues that women must
claim our power. Thus she argues that the liberating
tradition Ruether has discovered in the Bible is not
"usable" for women.

Elisabeth Schüssler Fiorenza in her recent book
In Memory of Her concurs with Christ's statement that
women cannot simply appropriate the liberating
tradition Ruether has discovered in the Bible. One
cannot, she agrees, abstract a liberating tradition
from the core of Christianity without being aware of
how that tradition has functioned within the history
of women. The attempt to argue for the "usability"
of the messianic-prophetic tradition for women's
empowerment draws, she states, "a rather idealized
picture of the biblical and prophetic traditions" and
"overlooks the oppressive androcentric elements of
these traditions."[31] But whereas
Schüssler-Fiorenza agrees with Christ that Ruether's
argument has not made the liberating tradition of
Christianity readily usable by women, she concurs
with Ruether that the messianic-prophetic tradition
can be used in the interest of feminism. "Without
question," she says, "this is the case. . . ."[32]
Without question the intent is there. But,
Schüssler-Fiorenza argues, it is not usable in the

41

form Ruether presents it. It is not usable as
abstracted from history. It is only usable when it
can be "historicized" within the history of women,
for it is history that empowers women. Thus,
Schüssler-Fiorenza describes her task as one of
reconstructing through a feminist hermeneutic of
suspicion that engages the Bible in a feminist way
the intertwining histories of Christianity and of
women in such a way that the suffering of women
throughout the tradition can be revealed. Yet, in
reconstructing the history of Christian origins from
the perspective of women's history,
Schüssler-Fiorenza discovers not only the suffering
of women, but also women's religious power. Women,
she argues, were central to the early Christian
movement and were persons of religious agency. They
were leaders and disciples as well as victims. By
reconstructing women's history in the midst of the
history of Christian origins, Schüssler-Fiorenza thus
discovers the "subversive memory"[33] of women's
history--a memory that she argues can be reclaimed to
empower women today. Thus in reconstructing women's
history and discovering women's central leadership
role in the Christian movement, she "historicizes"
the liberating tradition of Christianity in the
history of women and shows not "abstractly" but
"concretely" that the liberating tradition has been
used in women's history for women's liberation from
patriarchy--and thus can be usable by women today.
Asking the question: "Is it possible to read the
Bible in such a way that it becomes a historical
source and theological symbol for such power,
independence, and freedom?"[34] Schüssler-Fiorenza
answers that "the gospel can become again a 'power
for the salvation' of women as well as men."[35]

Although I concur with Christ and
Schüssler-Fiorenza that, in claiming the "usability"
of the liberating tradition within Christianity, one
must be aware of how that tradition has functioned
historically, I do not agree with Schüssler-Fiorenza
that the liberating intention is only usable by women
when it is "concretized" in women's history.
Theological symbols or traditions such as the one
Ruether has discovered, I would argue, can be used by
women. As Ruether suggests,[36] Mary Daly's use of
"the basic paradigm of classical theology" in her
Beyond God the Father proves the point. Daly,
Ruether argues, appropriates this very paradigm in
envisioning women's liberation and in announcing "a

42

prophetic, critical, or transformative mission against sinful society."[37] However, Schüssler-Fiorenza's historical work makes the liberating tradition discovered by Ruether <u>more</u> usable, offering women not only a tradition that <u>is</u> liberating in a general way, but also a history in which that tradition has been used against patriarchal oppression.

Let us turn then to the work of Schüssler-Fiorenza and her reconstruction of Christian origins to see how the history of women in Christianity reveals the usability of Christianity for the liberation of women. Women, she argues, were central to the early Christian tradition; they were the faithful disciples of Jesus; and as missionaries and leaders of house churches, they held positions of authority in the early Church. Against a patriarchal orthodoxy that has denied women a central leadership position in the Church, Schüssler-Fiorenza shows that women's leadership was part of the apostolic tradition. Christianity, as Schüssler-Fiorenza reconstructs its origins, is concerned with liberation, and her intent is to recover <u>that history</u> of liberation.

In the early Christian movement, Schüssler-Fiorenza argues, women were agents, subjects, leaders. Moreover, "the reality of women's engagement and leadership in these movements precedes the androcentric injunctions for women's role and behavior."[38] Women were leaders and full participants in early Christian communities and the androcentric (and misogynist) tradition that we know of as Christianity is not the only voice within the Christian tradition. In fact, various texts that speak of women's confinement, Schüssler-Fiorenza notes, need not be understood as descriptive of women's actual history but rather can be seen as the response of patriarchal leaders seeking to constrain women's actual participation. She notes: "The androcentric selection and transmission of early Christian traditions have manufactured the historical marginality of women. . . ."[39] But really "women had the power and authority of the gospel."[40] Thus, she charges, "insofar as the writings collected and accepted in the New Testament canon were selected and codified by the patristic New Testament church, the canon is a record of the 'historical winners.'"[41] However, these traditions "are not a

43

reflection of the early historical reality of women's leadership and participation in the early Christian movement."[42] Rather, Christian history "must be reconstituted as a history of liberation and of religious agency" of women.[43]

Although Krister Stendahl has been quoted on the jacket cover of Schüssler-Fiorenza's book saying that her work is "fully within the common standards of biblical scholarship," there have been some murmurings about whether the reconstructed Christian origin she proposes is accurate.[44] For the purposes of this book, however, although it is important that Schüssler-Fiorenza's work be convincing (meaning that her reconstruction is both a convincing vision of Christianity and a plausible reconstruction of the events of early Christianity), it is not necessary that it be vindicated as historically accurate in every detail. The concern in this book is whether her reconstructed Christian tradition can in fact empower women today. If it can, then perhaps the Christian community, developed along the trajectory of Schüssler-Fiorenza's reconstruction, can become an environment today for the encouragement of women towards our liberation.[45]

Whether expressed in the language of the "basileia of God," (kingdom of God) which was characteristic of the Jesus movement in Palestine, or in the vision of the "new creation," which was characteristic of the Christian movement in the Greco-Roman cities, Christianity, Schüssler-Fiorenza argues, was concerned with liberation--with the restoration of human wholeness that was an inbreaking possibility in the present. In her interpretation, "not the holiness of the elect but the wholeness of all is the central vision of Jesus."[46] The "salvation of God's basileia is present and experientially available whenever Jesus casts out demons (Luke 11:20), heals the sick and the ritually unclean, tells stories about the lost who are found, of the uninvited who are invited, or of the last who will be first."[47] Thus, "Jesus' praxis and vision of the basileia is the mediation of God's future into the structures and experiences of his own time and people."[48] Jesus offered a healing, a wholeness, that was not a disembodied holiness. Neither was it a distant vision; instead it was a present possibility. And this wholeness, Schüssler-Fiorenza argues, applies to women as well. "His healings and

44

exorcisms make women whole. His announcement of 'eschatological reversals'--many who are first will be last and those last will be first--applies also to women and to their impairment by patriarchal structures."[49] Jesus, Schüssler-Fiorenza argues, was in fact concerned to effect liberation from patriarchal structures. While "the prescription of the Holiness Code, as well as the scribal regulations, controlled women's lives even more than men's lives, and more stringently determined their access to God's presence in Temple and Torah,"[50] she notes that Jesus and his movement

> . . . offered an alternative interpretation of the Torah that opened up access to God for everyone who was a member of the elect people of Israel, and especially for those who, because of their societal situation, had little chance to experience God's power in Temple and Torah.[51]

She notes, "Jesus' proclamation does not address critically the structures of oppression."[52] Yet, she argues, Jesus' proclamation "implicitly subverts them by envisioning a different future and different human relationships on the grounds that all persons in Israel are created and elected by the gracious goodness of Jesus' Sophia-God."[53]

Schüssler-Fiorenza argues that Jesus implicitly, by offering human wholeness to all alike, subverted a patriarchal system that confined people and cut them off from their wholeness. But, Jesus also questioned the patriarchal structure of society more explicity in three ways. First, he challenged the patriarchal marriage structure. Jesus, she argues, refused to presuppose patriarchal marriage as a "given." Rather, in the basileia--in God's world--"'patriarchal marriage is no more,' because its function in maintaining and continuing patriarchal economic and religious structures is no longer necessary."[54] The God of Jesus did not condone or establish patriarchal structures. Israel's promise was "not guaranteed in and through patriarchal marriage structures, but through the promise and faithfulness of Israel's powerful, life-giving God."[55] The "God of the patriarchal systems and its securities is the 'God of the dead,' [but] the God of Israel is 'the God of the living.'"[56] Thus, according to

Schüssler-Fiorenza's interpretation, "in God's world women and men no longer relate to each other in terms of patriarchal dominance and dependence but as persons who live in the presence of the living God."[57] The basileia of God announced by Jesus was one where women and men relate as equals, not confined by patriarchally defined gender roles.

Moreover, Schüssler-Fiorenza argues, Jesus questioned the patriarchal structure of society through the "a-familial" ethos of the Jesus movement."[58] When in Luke 11:27 a bystander blesses the womb that bore Jesus, Jesus' response indicates that "faithful discipleship, not biological motherhood, is the eschatological calling of women."[59] Moreover, she notes, Jesus considered his true family to be not his biological family but rather "those who live the gracious goodness of God. . . ."[60] Yet what Schüssler-Fiorenza suggests is even more subversive is that when Jesus spoke about his true family, it "includes brothers, sisters, and mothers, but, significantly enough, no fathers."[61] Thus she concludes, "the discipleship community abolishes the claims of the patriarchal family and constitutes a new familial community, one that does not include fathers in its circle."[62]

Thirdly, Schüssler-Fiorenza argues, Jesus questioned the patriarchal structure of society in his insistence that relationships in the community of disciples be domination free.

This new "family" of equal discipleship, however, has no room for "fathers." Whereas "fathers" are mentioned among those left behind, they are not included in the new kinship which the disciples acquire "already now in this time." Insofar as the new "family" of Jesus has no room for "fathers," it implicitly rejects their power and status and thus claims that in the messianic community all patriarchal structures are abolished. Rather than reproducing the patriarchal relationships of the "household" in antiquity, the Jesus movement demands a radical break from it.[63]

Furthermore, Jesus' saying that "whoever does not receive the basileia of God like a child (slave)

46

shall not enter it," was "a challenge to relinquish
all claims of power and domination over others" and
become like a child (slave).[64] This saying, she
notes, "challenged all those in Palestine who were
prominent in their society to be in 'solidarity' with
the slaves and powerless in Israel."[65] Thus she
argues that the basileia of God

> . . . presupposes a society in which
> masters and slaves exist, and challenges
> those in positions of dominance . . . to
> become "equal" with those who are
> powerless. Masters should relinquish
> domination over their slaves and tenants
> and "serve" them in the same total fashion
> as a slave had to serve her/his master.[66]

Thus, Schüssler-Fiorenza argues that Jesus
directly challenged the patriarchal structures of
society by calling people into a community of equals
where there was no domination and where "those who
'would be' great or first among the disciples must be
slaves and servants of all."[67] In solidarity with
the dominated, those who entered this new community
became servants of each other. In this new community
of equals where each served the other in solidarity
with their needs, a new human wholeness was
experienced.

Jesus further subverted the patriarchal system,
Schüssler-Fiorenza argues, by calling God "father."
Whereas contemporary feminists argue that the
fatherhood of God reinforces patriarchal structures,
Schüssler-Fiorenza argues that "the 'father' God is
invoked here . . . not to justify patriarchal
structures and relationships in the community of
disciples but precisely to reject all such claims,
powers, and structures."[68] This is not to say that
Schüssler-Fiorenza does not affirm that the
fatherhood of God has been used exactly as
contemporary feminists charge, however. But, in the
basileia announced by Jesus, only God is to be
"father" and thus the members are freed from
patriarchal submission to human fathers. She
concludes:

> The "father" God of Jesus makes possible
> "the sisterhood of men" (in the phrase of
> Mary Daly) by denying any father, and all
> patriarchy, its right to existence.

47

Neither the "brothers" nor the "sisters" in the Christian community can claim the "authority of the father" because that would involve claiming authority and power reserved for God alone.[69]

Moreover, Schüssler-Fiorenza suggests that the God of Jesus subverted the patriarchal system because this God was a God Jesus' contemporaries would have recognized, through the nature of the divine all-inclusive love, as Sophia--"Israel's God in the language and Gestalt of the goddess."[70] Just as the God of Jesus "is a God of graciousness and goodness who accepts everyone and brings about justice and well being for everyone without exception"[71]--just as Jesus describes the action of God as being "like the man searching for his lost sheep, like the woman tirelessly sweeping for her lost coin,"[72] so Schüssler-Fiorenza argues, the people of Jesus' day would have known that God as Sophia, who is called by the tradition

> . . . sister, wife, mother, beloved, and teacher. She is the leader on the way, the preacher in Israel, the taskmaster and creator God. She seeks people, finds them on the road, invites them to dinner. She offers life, rest, knowledge, and salvation to those who accept her. Sophia dwells in Israel and officiates in the sanctuary. She sends prophets and apostles and makes those who accept her "friends of God." "She is but one but yet can do everything, herself unchanging. She makes all things new" (Wis 7:27). . . . She is described as "all-powerful, intelligent, unique" (Wis 7:22). She is a people-loving spirit who shares the throne of God (9:10). She is an initiate (mystis) of God's knowledge, an associate in God's works, and emanation of the God of light, who lives in symbiosis with God (8:3-4), an image of God's goodness (7:26).[73]

It is, Schüssler-Fiorenza argues, Sophia (and not a patriarchal male god) that the people would have recognized as the God of Jesus. She states:

> The earliest Palestinian theological remembrances and interpretations of Jesus'

life and death understand him as Sophia's messenger and later as Sophia herself. The earliest Christian theology is sophialogy. It was possible to understand Jesus' ministry and death in terms of God-Sophia, because Jesus probably understood himself as the prophet and child of Sophia.[74]

Thus she concludes:

. . . the Palestinian Jesus movement understands the ministry and mission of Jesus as that of the prophet and child of Sophia sent to announce that God is the God of the poor and heavy laden, of the outcasts and those who suffer injustice. As child of Sophia he stands in a long line and succession of prophets sent to gather the children of Israel to their gracious Sophia-God.[75]

Moreover, the understanding that the God of Jesus was one whom the people knew to be Sophia-God, one who "wills the wholeness and humanity of everyone" further emphasizes that the community called forth by Jesus was to become a "discipleship of equals."[76] The God who Jesus called "father," thereby challenging patriarchal/hierarchial systems, was also the Sophia-God who "offers life, rest, knowledge, and salvation to those who accept her," thereby calling Jesus' disciples to follow "the same praxis of inclusiveness and equality lived by Jesus-Sophia."[77] They are "sent to make the basileia experientially available in their healings and exorcisms, by restoring the humanity and wholeness of Sophia-God's children."[78] Thus Schüssler-Fiorenza concludes:

What they offered was not an alternative life style but an alternative ethos: they were those without a future, but now they had hope again; they were the "outcast" and marginal people in their society, but now they had community again; they were despised and downtrodden, but now they had dignity and self-confidence as God-Sophia's beloved children; they were, because of life's circumstances and social injustices, sinners with no hope to share in the holiness and presence of God, but now they

49

were heirs of the basileia, experiencing
the gracious goodness of God who had made
them equal to the holy and righteous in
Israel.[79]

The basileia vision of the early Jesus movement,
Schüssler-Fiorenza declares, was one that called
persons into a community where the disciples were all
to be equal, where none was to exercise patriarchal
prerogatives over another, and where each one was to
express solidarity with the others by becoming not a
master but a servant. This vision was not only a
future hope but a present reality for those who
joined the early Christian movement. These early
Christian communities were ones, she insists, in
which the inclusive vision of the baptismal statement
of Gal 3:28 ("There is neither Jew nor Greek, there
is neither slave nor free, there is neither male nor
female; for you are all one in Christ Jesus.") was
central and in fact an actuality. Women were equal
participants not only in the basileia vision but in
the actuality of the early communities as well.

Women's leadership in the early Christian
missionary movement that followed the early
Palestinian Jesus movement, Schüssler-Fiorenza
suggests, was more evident than androcentric biblical
texts would indicate. While the book of Acts and the
letters of Paul would seem to suggest that Paul was
the center of the early Christian missionary
movement, Schüssler-Fiorenza suggests that the early
movement was probably more diverse, and that women
were prominent leaders and missionaries in this
movement "both before Paul and independently of
Paul."[80] Women were not, she argues, peripheral to
the early Christian missionary movement. They became
a part of these early communities of equals and
participated with equality in various leadership
roles--most particularly as missionaries and as
leaders of churches that met in their homes.
Moreover, women missionaries such as Prisca were
Paul's co-workers (not his subordinates) and she
herself "was independent of the apostle and did not
stand under his authority."[81] Although the type of
leadership exercised in this early Christian
missionary movement did not mean power over anyone
else and prestige in the "patriarchal" sense but was
really a form of caring for others,
Schüssler-Fiorenza argues that participation in this
movement "allowed those who were socially and

politically marginal--because they were women--to gain new dignity and status."[82]

Participating as equals in a community that offered an alternative to the patriarchal ethos, women were able to discover a sense of self-worth and empowerment.

> Christ is preached to Jews and Greeks as "the power of God" and "the sophia of God" (1 Cor 1:24). Therefore he is the Lord of glory, the Lord is the Spirit (Sophia) and the liberator (wherever the Spirit of the Lord is, there is freedom; cf. 2 Cor 3:17). The <u>basileia</u> of God does not consist in "mere talk" but in "power" (1 Cor 4:20).[83]

This is the power, Schüssler-Fiorenza argues, to become a new creation. "Those who have entered the force field of the resurrected Lord, the liberating Wisdom (2 Cor 3:17)," she argues, knew they had been

> . . . set free "to share in the glorious freedom of the children of God" (Rom 8:21). The life-giving power of the resurrected Lord has called forth a new creation, in the midst of this death-ridden world, the <u>sarx</u>. Therefore Paul can proclaim, "Behold, now is the day of salvation" (2 Cor 6:2), and define the gospel "as God's power for salvation to everyone who has faith" (Rom 1:16).[84]

In this community the "newness" entered time and marked "the beginning of a new epoch" in which death is transformed into life--which means for Schüssler-Fiorenza that the old ways of living that deny full humanity to people, especially women, are transformed through the power of God and new life is made possible. "Christ-Sophia has appeared in the midst of this old world of death and alienation in order to fashion a new people, 'the sons and daughters of God.'"[85] These brothers and sisters through baptism are

> . . . "a new creation," the Spirit-filled people, those who have been purified, sanctified, and justified. They all are equal, because they all share in the

Spirit, God's power; they are all called elect and holy because they are adopted by God, all without exception: Jews, pagans, women, men, slaves, free poor, rich, those with high status and those who are "nothing" in the eyes of the world.[86]

Thus she argues:

Gal 3:28 belongs to this theological setting and missionary environment. It is not a Pauline "peak formulation" or a theological breakthrough achieved by Paul, or an occasional, isolated statement of Paul that is outnumbered by the subordination passages. Gal 3:28 is a key expression, not of Pauline theology but of the theological self-understanding of the Christian missionary movement which had far-reaching historical impact.[87]

For Schüssler-Fiorenza this theological self-understanding has had "far-reaching historical impact" because the vision of Gal 3:28 existed historically in early Christian communities--communities that suffered because they insisted on living this alternative ethos in the midst of patriarchal pressure to conform to the societal structures surrounding them. "As an alternative association which accorded women- and slave-initiates equal status and roles, the Christian missionary movement was a conflict movement which stood in tension with the institutions of slavery and the patriarchal family."[88] Rather than conform to the patriarchal way of life, Christians, Schüssler-Fiorenza argues, were a people freed to a new life.[89] "The goal of the Christian calling," she asserts, "is freedom: 'You were called to a freedom' (Gal 5:13), because 'where the Spirit of the Lord is there is freedom' (2 Cor 3:17)."[90] "Liberation from the slavery of sin, law, and death, from the conditions of the 'present evil age' (Gal 1:4) has 'freedom' as its purpose and destiny."[91] "As a result," Schüssler-Fiorenza quotes H. D. Betz, "eleutheria (freedom) is the central theological concept which sums up the Christian's situation before God as well as in this world."[92] This freedom is reflected in the formula of Gal 3:28 for "it proclaims that in the Christian community all distinctions of religion, race, class, nationality, and gender are insignificant."[93] People were freed from the old divisions and names that had supported structures of domination to a new creation where distinctions were insignificant and domination was no more.

But, Schüssler-Fiorenza argues, the affirmation of freedom and equality found in Gal 3:28 did not withstand the pressure of the patriarchal world. The vision of Gal 3:28 was modified by Paul, the Pauline school, and post-Pauline writers. This modification resulted in the gradual limitation of women's leadership roles in the churches. Instead of affirming that there were no patriarchal gender assignments in the new Christian community, patriarchal marriage arangements came to be reinforced and women's leadership roles narrowed to the confines of women's world. Moreover, she notes, Paul himself opened "the door for the reintroduction of patriarchal authority within the Christian community" through his claim to "spiritual" fatherhood for those he had converted.[94] Schüssler-Fiorenza argues: "By this 'spiritual' fatherhood he allows for an understanding of the Christian community as the 'new family of God' that has 'fathers' here on earth, not just one and only one 'father' in heaven."[95]

Schüssler-Fiorenza does note, however, some ambiguity within Paul's teachings on the issue of women's leadership. Since he did advise women to "remain free of the marriage bond" he can be seen as making a "frontal assualt on the intentions of existing law and the general cultural ethos. . . ."[96] She notes that this is in tension with his teachings of women's subordination within patriarchal marriages. Thus,

. . . Paul's impact on women's leadership in the Christian missionary movement is double-edged. On the one hand he affirms Christian equality and freedom. He opens up a new independent lifestyle for women by encouraging them to remain free of the bondage of marriage. On the other hand, he subordinates women's behavior in marriage and in the worship assembly to the interests of Christian mission, and restricts their rights not only as "pneumatics" but also as "women," for we do

53

not find such explicit restrictions on the
behavior of men _qua_ men in the worship
assembly.[97]

Schüssler-Fiorenza thus argues that the Bible
bears witness to a gradual patriarchalization process
in the Christian tradition as the early Christian
community eventually surrendered to the pressure
exerted upon it by the surrounding patriarchal
society. The teachings of Paul and the post-Pauline
writers reflect a transition from the alternative
Christian community characterized by the discipleship
of equals to one that affirmed the patriarchal
ethos--replacing "the genuine Christian vision of
equality" with the "patriarchal-societal ethos of the
time. . . ."[98] Such a transition tended to
spiritualize or internalize the Christian calling
characterizing it "as a purely religious calling that
does not disrupt the established order of the house
and state."[99] This transition is reflected as well
in the shift of authority in the early communities.
Gradually, she notes, the communities changed from
"house church" to "church as the 'household of God'"
with patriarchal fathers assuming the role of
leaders.[100] In time, she argues, a strain of
orthodoxy became "victorious" over other strains that
were labeled unorthodox or heretical with the
unfortunate result that "the patristic boundaries no
longer established Christian identity over and
against its patriarchal society but over and against
other Christian social and doctrinal systems."[101]
Thus women were removed from the center of Christian
tradition.

Yet because the early fathers spoke against
women's equality and argued in favor of the system of
patriarchy, Schüssler-Fiorenza, as noted before,
argues that it is incorrect to assume that the
teachings against women's equality and leadership
were at all descriptive of women's role in the early
communities. Rather, they more likely reflect the
patriarchal reaction to women's actual equality and
leadership. We know that women were leaders in the
Montanist and Gnostic movements as well as--as
attested to in the Bible--in the early Christain
missionary movement. And this, Schüssler-Fiorenza
argues, is but "the tip of an iceberg," for it points
to the roles that women really did play in the origin
of the Christian tradition. Not only, she says, were
women equal and leaders in the early Christian

movement, but also it is the women who served as "paradigms of true discipleship."[102]

And even as the early Church was patriarchalizing, Schüssler-Fiorenza maintains, not all early Christian communities surrendered to this process. Moreover, the "memory" of these non-patriarchalized communities bears witness to the very central role women played as equal disciples. Whereas the writers who accommodated patriarchal pressure "seek to stabilize the socially volatile situation of coequal discipleship by insisting on patriarchal dominance and submission structures, not only for the household but also for the church," Schüssler-Fiorenza argues, "the original Gospel writers move to the other end of the social 'balance' scale."[103] This they do by insisting "on altruistic behavior and service as the appropriate praxis and ethos of Christian leadership."[104] The Gospels of Mark and John, she argues, were written around the same time that Colossians and the Pastorals were being written from the patriarchal perspective, and they were written to actual communities emphasizing "service and love as the core of Jesus' ministry and as the central demand of discipleship."[105] Thus, Schüssler-Fiorenza argues, these New Testament writings reflect an alternative Christian reaction to the pressure of patriarchalization.

The Gospel of Mark, Schüssler-Fiorenza observes, centers on the importance of suffering in the teaching of Jesus. To a community that was resisting the pressure of patriarchalization, the Markan Jesus "clearly states that giving offense and experiencing suffering must not be shunned. A true disciple of Jesus must expect suffering, hatred, and persecution."[106] But, she adds, "suffering is not an end in itself . . . but is the outcome of Jesus' life-praxis of solidarity with the social and religious outcasts of his society."[107] That is, Jesus' suffering and that of true disciples comes from becoming equal to others (in solidarity with them) and making their cause his own. True disciples are those who "become the least, that is, the servants of all."[108] Jesus stresses

. . . that while pagan leadership is based on power and domination of others, among Christians such patriarchal relationships

55

of dominance are prohibited. The leaders
of the community must be servants of all
and those who are preeminent must become
slaves of all.[109]

Equality, Schüssler-Fiorenza argues, "is to be
achieved through altruism, through the placing of
interests of others and of the community
first."[110] And this form of community--this style
of leadership--she suggests was the cause of offense
to the dominant patriarchal society and led to the
community's suffering. "Domination-free leadership
in the community and being prepared to undergo
sufferings and persecutions are interconnected."[111]

Not only does the Gospel of Mark reflect an
alternative Christian community and an alternative
way of leadership, Schüssler-Fiorenza argues, but it
portrays women, and not the leading males, as the
true disciples. Women are the ones who follow Jesus
to the cross. They are the ones who "take the last
place on the community's social scale and exercise
their leadership as servitude."[112] They were "the
apostolic eyewitnesses of Jesus' death, burial, and
resurrection."[113] They are those who like Jesus do
"not subordinate and enslave others in the manner of
gentile rulers" but who are "the suffering servant
who liberates and elevates them from servitude."[114]

The Gospel of John, in a similar fashion,
focuses on the notion of true discipleship as
altruism and service. The Johannine community is one
of "friends" who practice alternative service and
love for each other. Women are shown as the true
disciples--"they are not just paradigms of faithful
discipleship to be initated by women but by all those
who belong to Jesus' 'very own' familial
community."[115] "Whereas the authors of the
Epistles appeal to the authority of Paul or Peter to
legitimize their injunctions for submission and
adaptation to Greco-Roman patriarchal structures,"
Schüssler-Fiorenza concludes

. . . the writers of the primary Gospels
appeal to Jesus himself to support their
alternative stress on altruistic love and
service, which is demanded not from the
least and the slaves but from the leaders
and the masters--and I might add, not only
from the women but also from the men.[116]

Schüssler-Fiorenza has reconstructed Christian origins to show how women very probably were central to the original Christian movement. Freed by the liberating work of Jesus from the power of patriarchy to enter a new creation--an alternative community where the greatest became least, women, Schüssler-Fiorenza argues, were transformed from marginal creatures to central figures in the work of the gospel. As such, she observes, they are remembered in the Gospels as "true disciples" who served and suffered for their ministry. Therefore she concludes:

> . . . wherever the gospel is preached and heard, promulgated and read, what the women have done is not totally forgotten because the Gospel story remembers that the discipleship and apostolic leadership of women are integral parts of Jesus' "alternative" praxis of <u>agape</u> and service.[117]

This subversive memory of women's central role in the origin of Christianity, Schüssler-Fiorenza maintains, can empower women to

> . . . build a feminist movement not on the fringes of church but as the central embodiment and incarnation of the vision of church that lives in solidarity with the oppressed and the impoverished, the majority of whom are women and children dependent on women.[118]

It is a memory that can empower a

> . . . feminist Christian spirituality . . . [which] calls us to gather together the <u>ekklesia of women</u> who, in the angry power of the Spirit, are sent forth to feed, heal, and liberate our own people who are women. . . . It sets us free from the internalization of false altruism and self-sacrifice that is concerned with the welfare and work of men first to the detriment of our own and other women's welfare and calling. It enables us to live "for one another" and to experience the presence of God in the <u>ekklesia</u> as the gathering of women.[119]

57

Schüssler-Fiorenza thus offers a reconstructed tradition--a tradition that shows women as leaders, true disciples, apostolic witnesses. She has re-opened the history of Christian origins and discovered through her reconstruction that women played central roles in the early Christian movement. She has argued that women (and others who were members of the <u>basileia</u> Jesus envisioned) suffered for living transformed lives in the community of the new creation. Moreover, she has suggested that the movement to patriarchalize Christianity was one that reacted against the very non-patriarchalized roles women were playing in the early Christian communities. Thus, she has pictured the history of early Christianity as one in which the process of patriarchalization produced suffering for women--not just as patriarchal "victims" but as "losers" in a struggle that led to the creation of new/old confinements, denying women what had been their own empowerment. She thus offers contemporary women a memory of the "sufferings, struggles and powers" of early Christian foresisters. And inasmuch as Judy Chicago is correct in arguing that "our heritage is our power,"[120] then Schüssler-Fiorenza is offering contemporary women a new source of empowerment that can transform Christian religious history "into a new liberating future. . . ."[121] This is a history that can empower women to gather as the <u>ekklesia</u> of women "to claim our own religious powers to participate fully in the decision-making process of church, and to nurture each other as women Christians."[122]

Schüssler-Fiorenza thus has shown how early Christianity was non-patriarchal and how the messianic-prophetic tradition was in fact used directly and indirectly to challenge the surrounding patriarchal society. The alternative Christian tradition she has reconstructed is one that has challenged patriarchal structures and recognized the full participation of women as equals and as persons of leadership and decision. The Jesus who, she has argued, called women from patriarchal submissive roles to new life in an egalitarian society, and a God who liberates the oppressed (and who can be seen as Sophia--"Israel's God in the language and <u>Gestalt</u> of the goddess.")[123] would indeed seem to be usable against patriarchy. Thus we can reply to our earlier question whether Christianity is necessarily patriarchal that Christianity is <u>not</u> necessarily patriarchal. Christianity, when it is true to the trajectory established in its early prototypical communities, is non-patriarchal. Thus in "historicizing" the prophetic-messianic tradition in women's history Schüssler-Fiorenza has affirmed that Christianity has been "usable" by women in our struggle against patriarchy. She thus makes it possible for us to ask in the next chapter whether or not this usable tradition can in fact be empowering to women in our liberation today.

In her Epilogue, Schüssler-Fiorenza argues that the alternative vision of Christianity she has reconstructed is liberating to women because it posits an egalitarian community where all could be leaders and where women could participate in decisions about our own welfare. Thus she posits an "ekklesia of women" where women are "free to choose an alternative life for ourselves and for each other."[124] It is a community where she envisions women working for our own cause in solidarity with all women. This ekklesia of women where women live for our own cause is in a sense the contemporary feminist movement. In showing how Christianity was in its origin a movement for liberation and equality, Schüssler-Fiorenza attempts to draw the feminist movement down to its Christian roots--thereby both empowering the feminist movement and Christianizing the feminist movement as well. She says: "Radical feminism has rediscovered the 'equality from below' espoused by the Jesus movement in Palestine without recognizing its religious roots."[125] Schüssler-Fiorenza is thus entwining ancient Christianity and modern feminism around each other, affirming that the feminist movement is rooted in Christianity, and that the Bible, can be read "in such a way that it becomes a historical source and theological symbol for such power, independence, and freedom."[126]

But while Schüssler-Fiorenza's project is thus in sympathy with the project of this book, it does not deal with the same question. My concern is to ask whether women can be empowered by Christianity to speak in our own voices, not whether women who are speaking in their own voices through the feminist movement can find further empowerment through the rediscovery of our roots in the early Christian tradition. In order to determine whether or not Christianity can in fact empower women to speak in

59

our own voices, then, I suggest we consider the way in which Schüssler-Fiorenza has characterized the early Christian community to see if these characteristics would in fact be liberating to women who have yet to speak in their own voices.

Schüssler-Fiorenza has characterized this early Christian community as "a discipleship of equals" where women and others were leaders--and as one in which "service" and "altruism" and "the placing of interests of others and of the community first" were of prime concern. In asking whether or not the Christianity Schüssler-Fiorenza has reconstructed is a Christianity that can empower women today, we must be aware that there is a dual movement at work in her book. On the one hand, she identifies the early Christian movement as one within a patriarchal society that called persons to be liberated into a new egalitarian society--a community in which the marginal, especially the women, could be leaders and decision-makers--persons of agency. On the other hand, she talks about the character of that leadership and of the relationship between members of the community as one of service and altruism--of a putting of the interests of others and the community first. Whereas she has largely affirmed that the claim that the "greatest should be least" is directed not to the "least and the slaves" but to "the leaders and the masters" (most of whom we can presume in a patriarchal society would have been men), she adds: "Not only from the women but also from the men."[127] This I would suggest creates a confusion, for whereas from the first perspective women are among "the least and the slaves" liberated to a new equality and not among those called to servanthood, from the other perspective women are those leaders who are to be servants. Indeed, the true disciples Schüssler-Fiorenza points to are women as suffering servants. On the one hand she is reconstructing Christianity as a movement in which women were offered equality and liberation into a new state of self-esteem; on the other hand, she is affirming that equality means service and altruism--becoming servants of each other. When we combine the two movements together into one, it appears that Schüssler-Fiorenza is suggesting that people who were liberated into this new community were liberated into service of and altruism toward the interests of others. Although she has said that service and altruism do not apply to the "slaves and least" and that the "least" were liberated to a new future of empowerment, she doesn't characterize what the "least and slaves" should become in the community. Since there _is_ equality in the community, it would thus seem reasonable to assume that they would also become servants of the community as well. Thus, in asking whether Christianity can empower women to be liberated today (and arguing through Schüssler-Fiorenza who is the most current voice for the affirmative today) we must ask whether service and altruism and putting the interests of others and the community first (the characteristics of the proto-typical Christian community)--can be liberating for women today.

In testing the liberating possibility of Christianity for women by seeing whether service and altruism and putting the interests of others and the community first would in fact empower women to speak in our own voices, we need to be aware that for Schüssler-Fiorenza clearly the interests and concerns that are to be put first in the Christian community of liberation are the interests and concerns of those traditionally marginalized in a patriarchal society--particularly women. Members of the Christian community were and are to live in solidarity with and as friends to the marginalized and welcome them into a community where there would be no discrimination by race, sex, or ethnic origin. The altruism she is thus speaking of is not a "false altruism" (which is concerned, as noted earlier, with the "welfare and work of men first to the detriment of our own and other women's welfare and calling") but an altruism that enables women to live "for one another."[128]

In characterizing the Christian community by its service and altruism Schüssler-Fiorenza stands in consensus with a major strain of the Christian tradition that has understood service and altruism or love to be among the distinguishing marks of the Christian community.[129] She has of course qualified service and altruism with the understanding that the interests to be served would be those of the marginal, especially women. I propose however for the purposes of this book to bracket the question of who the others are that are to be served and whose interests are to be put first. Although Schüssler-Fiorenza assumes that service and altruism for the cause of women can be empowering to women, I

61

am skeptical about whether or not they would be liberating--whether, when the interests of others are put before the interests of the woman who is seeking her own liberation--even if they are the interests of other women or the interests of women in general--she can be empowered to exorcise from within herself the voices of others and begin to speak in her own voice.

Schüssler-Fiorenza has established that Christianity need not be patriarchal--and thus she has opened up the possibility that it can empower women in our struggle for liberation from patriarchy today. She has offered women a history and a dynamic vision of a community that can inform our struggle today. In asking the question of the liberating potential of Christianity in the way I propose to do--whether service and altruism can empower women to our liberation, to speak in our own voices--I am in actuality not so much testing the liberating potential of the history Schüssler-Fiorenza has offered us as I am asking[130] a more a-historical question. As argued earlier[130] I am assuming that theological symbols such as ways of characterizing the early Christian community--can be used by women--and in fact do inform women--as we journey towards our liberation. Because the metaphors of service and altruism have, as presented in this a-historical sense, been central motifs in the description of what Christianity is to be about for much of the tradition, by bracketing what cause service and altruism are to be informed by, it can be argued that I am in actuality testing more what impact a traditional view of Christianity can have on women's journey toward liberation than I am testing what impact the notions of service and altruism in the cause of the marginalized--especially women--can have. Moreover, because theological symbols--even if presented a-historically--inform our lives in the context of our lived history, and because the lived history of Western civilization since before the advent of Christianity has been patriarchal, then one could argue that service and altruism, without being qualified by the contextual statement "for the interests of the marginalized especially women" will always be in the context of patriarchy and will therefore always be a "false altruism" as Schüssler-Fiorenza has defined the term. It can be argued then that in treating service and altruism a-historically I am actually testing whether a more conventional patriarchal notion of service and

62

altruism--really the "false altruism"
Schüssler-Fiorenza talks about, can liberate women.
Whereas I would submit that this is true, I am also
questioning whether any servant or altruistic
behavior--when it is defined as putting the interests
of others (even if meaning other women or the cause
of women) and the community first can be other than a
false altruism.

In Chapter III, then, we shall take the
characteristics of the Christian community as
described here--service and altruism and putting the
interests of others and the community first--and see
if these characteristics can be liberating for
women. To do this, we must delve deeper into women's
experience, beyond the affirmation of Chapter I that
women's liberation means naming ourselves and
speaking in our own voices, to explore just how women
do become selves--how we learn to speak in our own
voices. Then we shall determine whether altruism and
service would in fact enhance the process of
liberation--of coming to speak in our own voices--as
we will have explored it. If, as I shall show in
Chapter III, service and altruism do not empower
women to our liberation, and if Schüssler-Fiorenza is
right that Christianity can empower women to our
liberation (if the Bible can be read "in such a way
that it becomes a historical source and theological
symbol"[131] for such liberation), then it would
appear to be evident that Christian experience should
be characterized in another way than by service and
altruism if this liberating potential is to be
realized. In Chapter V, then, we shall begin to
explore an alternative way to characterize Christian
experience.

[1]Jürgen and Elisabeth Moltmann, "Becoming Human in New Community" in The Commumity of Women and Men in the Church, ed. Constance F. Parvey (Philadelphia: Fortress Press, 1983), pp. 31-32.

[2]Pope Paul VI's argument against the ordination of women because women cannot resemble Jesus would seem to prove the point. See Naomi Goldenberg's argument in Changing of the Gods: Feminism and the End of Traditional Religions (Boston: Beacon Press, 1979), pp. 5-6.

[3]Carol P. Christ and Judith Plaskow in "Introduction" to Womanspirit Rising: A Feminist Reader in Religion ed. Christ and Plaskow (San Francisco: Harper & Row, 1979), pp. 9-11.

[4]Although not all "revolutionaries" are comfortable with the notion of Goddess (Daly for example resists any reification, male or female), the Goddess, as we have seen in Carol P. Christ's argument related in Chapter I, is seen as a spiritual source of women's empowerment. Much as Feuerbach argued that Christianity was the empowerment of humanity because in Christianity God became man (see The Essence of Christianity [New York: Harper & Row, 1957]) thus affirming that all the best human attributes which were projected upon the deity were possible for "men"--so these women argue that women through the Goddess find their own powers affirmed. As Ntozake Shange has written: "i found god in myself & i loved her / i loved her fiercely." Quoted in the Politics of Women's Spirituality, ed. Charlene Spretnak (Garden City: Anchor Press/Doubleday, 1982), p. 3.

[5]See Phyllis Trible, God and the Rhetoric of Sexuality (Philadelphia: Fortress Press, 1978).

[6]Both Russell and Ruether have written extensively on the subject. See in particular Russell's Human Liberation in a Feminist Perspective: A Theology (Philadelphia: The Westminster Press, 1974); and Ruether's Liberation Theology (New York: Paulist Press, 1972).

[7]See Letha Scanzoni and Nancy Hardesty, All We're Meant to Be: A Biblical Approach to Women's

<u>Liberation</u> (Waco, Texas: Word Books, 1974); as well as the work of Leonard and Arlene Swidler, and Virginia Ramey Mollenkott.

[8]Or "seed" as Mary Daly refers to it in her earliest book <u>The Church and the Second Sex</u> (New York: Harper & Row, 1968), the last chapter of which is entitled: "The Second Sex and the Seeds of Transcendence."

[9]Liberation theologies such as those of third-world theologian Gustave Gutierrez and black theologian James Cone claim as well that Christianity has at its core the liberating vision of a God who leads slaves out of Egypt, becomes incarnated to become one with the oppressed and set them free, and calls those who would be true disciples to "set at liberty the oppressed."

[10]Rosemary Radford Ruether, "A Religion for Women," <u>WomanSpirit</u> vol. 6, no. 24 (Summer 1980), p. 24. All back issues of <u>WomanSpirit</u> are available. Inquire from WomanSpirit, 200 King Mountain Trail, Wolf Creek, Oregon 97497.

[11]<u>Ibid.</u>, p. 24.

[12]<u>Ibid.</u>, p. 24.

[13]<u>Ibid.</u>, p. 24.

[14]<u>Ibid.</u>, p. 24.

[15]<u>Ibid.</u>, p. 24.

[16]<u>Ibid.</u>, p. 24.

[17]<u>Ibid.</u>, p. 24.

[18]<u>Ibid.</u>, p. 24.

[19]<u>Ibid.</u>, p. 24.

[20]<u>Ibid.</u>, p. 24.

[21]<u>Ibid.</u>, p. 24.

[22]<u>Ibid.</u>, p. 24.

[23]<u>Ibid.</u>, p. 24.

[24]Ibid., p. 24.

[25]Ibid., p. 24.

[26]Ibid., p. 24.

[27]Carol P. Christ, "Another Response to a Religion for Women," Womanspirit vol. 6, no. 24 (Summer 1980), p. 28.

[28]Ibid., p. 29. (underlinings Christ's)

[29]Ibid., p. 29.

[30]Ibid., p. 29.

[31]Elisabeth Schüssler Schüssler-Fiorenza, In Memory of Her: A Feminist Theological Reconstruction of Christian Origins (New York: Crossroad, 1983), p. 17.

[32]Ibid., p. 17.

[33]Ibid., p. 31.

[34]Ibid., p. 19.

[35]Ibid., p. 31.

[36]Rosemary Radford Ruether, Sexism and God-Talk: Toward a Feminist Theology (Boston: Beacon Press, 1983), p. 38.

[37]Ibid., p. 38.

[38]Schüssler-Fiorenza, p. 35.

[39]Ibid., p. 52.

[40]Ibid., p. 36.

[41]Ibid., p. 55.

[42]Ibid., p. 52.

[43]Ibid., p. 36.

[44]These murmurings were related to me in two conversations. One was with Ann Weir in February, 1984, and the other was with Ann Taves in April, 1984.

[45]Schüssler-Fiorenza's method suggests that the early Christian movement recorded in the New Testament is a "prototype"--a proto-model for the contemporary church. As a prototype it is "not a binding timeless pattern or principle" but is "critically open to the possibility of its own transformation." That is, this prototype can serve as a model that can move the current Christian community along the proto-typical trajectory. See p. 33.

[46]Ibid., p. 121.

[47]Ibid., pp. 120-121.

[48]Ibid., p. 121.

[49]Ibid., p 121.

[50]Ibid., p. 141.

[51]Ibid., p. 141.

[52]Ibid., p. 142.

[53]Ibid., p. 142. She continues: "Jesus and his movement set free those who are dehumanized and in bondage to evil powers, thus implicitly subverting economic or patriarchal-androcentric structures, even though the people involved in this process might not have thought in terms of social structures."

[54]Ibid., p. 144.

[55]Ibid., p. 145.

[56]Ibid., p. 145.

[57]Ibid., p. 145.

[58]Ibid., p. 143.

[59]Ibid., p. 146.

[60]Ibid., p. 147.

[61]Ibid., p. 147.

[62]Ibid., p. 147.

[63]Ibid., pp. 147-48.

[64]Ibid., p. 148.

[65]Ibid., p. 148.

[66]Ibid., p. 148.

[67]Ibid., p. 148.

[68]Ibid., p. 150.

[69]Ibid., p. 151.

[70]Ibid., p. 133.

[71]Ibid., p. 130.

[72]Ibid., p. 131.

[73]Ibid., p. 133.

[74]Ibid., p. 134.

[75]Ibid., p. 135. It is worth noting that Schüssler-Fiorenza's suggestion that Jesus was a child of Sophia suggests the interesting possibility that Jesus' divine nature--and that of the second person of the Christian Trinity--was feminine!

[76]Ibid., p. 135.

[77]Ibid., p. 135.

[78]Ibid., p. 135.

[79]Ibid., pp. 135-36.

[80]Ibid., p. 161.

[81]Ibid., p. 178.

[82]Ibid., p. 183.

[83]Ibid., p. 184.

[84]Ibid., p. 186.

[85]Ibid., pp. 198-99.

[86]Ibid., p. 199.

[87]Ibid., p. 199.

[88]Ibid., p. 216. Schüssler-Fiorenza makes a distinction between the community's suffering because it was a "new creation" persecuted by the "old," and suffering as the Pauline school understands it. "The Pauline school uses the cross as a symbol to justify religiously the suffering of those oppressed by the present order of slavery or patriarchy (thus 1 Peter and Colossians). Cross and suffering are no longer (emphasis mine) understood as the necessary outcome of the tension between the newness of God's vision and the new creation in Jesus Christ on the one hand and the old oppressive order of this world, which rules through suffering, sin, and death on the other." p. 187-88. For Schüssler-Fiorenza the cross and suffering are descriptive of what happens to persons who live in the new creation: they are persecuted and killed by the powers of death.

[89]Schüssler-Fiorenza points to freedom formulae in the Pauline letters to justify this point. "You were bought with a price, do not become human slaves" (1 Cor 6:20; 7:23). Or "For freedom Christ has set us free . . . do not submit again to a yoke of slavery" (Gal 5:1). See p. 209.

[90]Ibid., p. 209.

[91]Ibid., p. 209.

[92]Ibid., pp. 209-10. She quotes H. D. Betz's Galatians.

[93]Ibid., p. 213.

[94]Ibid., p. 234.

[95]Ibid., p. 234. Schüssler-Fiorenza adds however that although "Paul makes it possible for later generations to transfer the hierarchy of the patriarchal family to the new family of God . . . he himself certainly does not understand his authority and ministry as patriarchal, but as the nuturing, life-enhancing service of a nurse or a mother."

[96]Ibid., p. 225.

[97]Ibid., p. 236.

[98]Ibid., p. 266.

[99]Ibid., p. 266.

[100]Ibid., pp. 286-87.

[101]Ibid., p. 303.

[102]Ibid., p. 315.

[103]Ibid., p. 315-16.

[104]Ibid., p. 316.

[105]Ibid., p. 316. In this section of her book, Schüssler-Fiorenza sometimes uses the word "love" or the phrase "altruistic love" interchangeably with the term "altruism" or "altruistic behavior." Since the latter two terms are the ones she uses more consistently, and since she defines altruism--"Equality is to be achieved through altruism, through the placing of interests of others and of the community first" (p. 318, emphasis mine)--where there have been centuries of debate over how to define what is meant by "love" in Christian thought, I have chosen to use the term altruism in tandem with "service" or "servanthood" to speak about the characteristics of this early Christian community as Schüssler-Fiorenza has reconstructed it. Not all Christian thinkers have defined altruism or altruistic love as "placing of interests of others and of the community first." Daniel Day Williams, for example, (see Chapter IV) argues for a more mutual understanding of Christian love. See also Gene Outka's Agape: An Ethical Analysis (New Haven: Yale University Press, 1972).

[106]Ibid., p. 317.

[107]Ibid., p. 317.

[108]Ibid., p. 318.

[109]Ibid., p. 318.

[110]Ibid., p. 318.

[111]Ibid., p. 319.

[112]Ibid., p. 320.

[113]Ibid., p. 321.

[114]Ibid., p. 320.

[115]Ibid., p. 333.

[116]Ibid., p. 334.

[117]Ibid., p. 334.

[118]Ibid., p. 344.

[119]Ibid., p. 346.

[120]Ibid., p. xix.

[121]Ibid., p. xix.

[122]Ibid., p. 344.

[123]Ibid., p. 133.

[124]Ibid., pp. 344-45.

[125]Ibid., p. 132. Although I have referred to these roots as Christian since Schüssler-Fiorenza argues that the Jesus movement was a movement within Judaism, the roots are more correctly Judeo-Christian.

[126]Ibid., p. 19.

[127]Ibid., p. 334.

[128]Ibid., p. 346.

[129]For example: Mt 22:37-40 "Thou shalt love the Lord Thy God with all thy heart, and with all thy soul, and with all thy mind. This is the first and great commandment. And the second is like unto it, Thou shalt love thy neighbor as thyself. On these two commandments hang all the laws and the prophets." And I John 4:7-8 "Beloved let us love one another for love is of God, and those who love are born of God and know God. They who do not love do not know God; for God is love."

[130]See page 42.

131See page 59.

CHAPTER III

Altruism, Service, and the Convention of Feminine Goodness

We have seen in Chapter I that when women speak of liberation we mean our empowerment to name our oppression and begin to name ourselves from within ourselves, speaking from our own centers and in our own voices. The process of women's liberation begins with a woman's awareness that reality could be different from the way patriarchy has defined it. In becoming aware of such a possibility, women are awakened to the fact that our present situation is oppressive. The moment of awareness, I have suggested, reflects the emergence of a woman's consciousness, of her own perspective, and thus her own center. From this center of awareness she is then ready to risk naming herself toward a new reality. In beginning to name herself, the world, and--as Mary Daly suggests--in beginning to name toward God, a woman experiences her full human freedom. This freedom is the freedom to name, create, and weave from her own center of being. While women may use the words freedom and autonomy, we have seen that contemporary feminists such as Robin Morgan and Catherine Keller are defining those terms in a "feminist" way. Freedom and autonomy refer to women's human creativity and center of agency--our ability to participate in the ongoing processing of reality in a creative way. But freedom and autonomy are also deeply contextual. Freedom lives in the connections, Morgan has affirmed. Freedom is not cut off and unaffected. It is deeply grounded in connection and exists in the midst of connectivity.

In Chapter II we have explored the possibility that Christianity might be a source of empowerment in women's struggle for liberation. Although Christianity has served through much of its history as a patriarchal religion, reinforcing patriarchal social structures, we have considered the claims of Rosemary Ruether and Elisabeth Schüssler-Fiorenza that the gospel can become a source of empowerment for women in our journey towards liberation. Schüssler-Fiorenza, in awareness of the critique leveled against Christianity by other feminists, has reconstructed the history of Christian origins in such a way, she feels, that it can empower women.

73

She has argued that Christianity can encourage women to name our oppression, for she has shown how the basileia vision of Jesus and the early Christian community itself were a challenge to the dominant patriarchal society. In this new community, she argues, women were equals. They had equal access to positions of leadership and thus would have been involved in making decisions for the community. Thus she has shown how women were encouraged to leave their oppressive state and enter a community in which they found religious agency. Moreover, she has argued that the God of Jesus was not only "non-patriarchal" but also a God who sought to make people friends of God, calling them to their wholeness as human creatures. This God, she argues, was and can be in the "Gestalt of the goddess"--a God who calls people, especially women, to our empowerment. Thus Schüssler-Fiorenza argues that the gospel and any Christian community that follows the trajectory of the proto-typical community she has reconstructed--any community that lives in solidarity with the stories of the women she has retold--can empower women today. The gospel, she argues, can encourage women to name our oppression and to participate as equals and leaders, persons of agency and wholeness, in the transformation of the world and the Church beyond our patriarchal bindings.

Schüssler-Fiorenza has thus offered to women a history--a Biblical history--that can empower women today. But in determining whether or not Christianity can be a source of empowerment for women in our struggle for liberation, I have asked whether not only the history Schüssler-Fiorenza has reconstructed but also the theological symbols that characterize that Christian community can empower women today. Schüssler-Fiorenza has described the early Christian community as one of a "discipleship of equals" where women were leaders--a community whose service and altruism, putting the needs of others and the community first, were characteristic. Thus I have suggested that in this chapter we test the characteristics of service and altruism, as thus described, in the context of women's experience to see whether they can serve as theological symbols that can be a source of empowerment for women's liberation. Although Schüssler-Fiorenza has argued that the service and altruism of the Christian community were and are to be for the needs of those usually marginalized in a patriarchal

74

society--particularly women--I have suggested that we bracket for the purposes of this book the question of who the others are whose needs are to be attended to first. This is because I suspect that any attitude of service and altruism when they mean putting the needs of others and the community first, will mean for women not liberation but a "false altruism" that by definition works to the detriment of women's welfare. In this chapter we shall test out this suspicion and ask whether the call to service and altruism, putting the needs of others and the community first, can empower women's liberation from patriarchy today. Can it empower women to speak in our own voices and to challenge patriarchal systems that keep us confined within limited roles--roles that largely have to do with our relationships to men and to our children?

To answer these questions, let us return to women's experience and explore more fully how women come to speak in our own voices. Nancy Chodorow, we have seen in Chapter I, has shown that growing girls develop differently from growing boys and come to define themselves as continuous with others.[1] "Their experience of self," she states, "contains more flexible or permeable ego boundaries"[2] than those experienced by boys. This means that in exploring whether or not Christianity as characterized by service and altruism can empower women, we must explore what is known specifically of women's experience. The emphasis on women's experience is crucial. One of the issues raised by the sources used in this chapter is that what has been called "human" experience has in fact been male experience. Since these sources argue that women's experience is in fact different from male experience, we can only test whether service and altruism are empowering to women in the context of experience that is self-consciously women's. The purpose of this chapter is to explore women's experience and ask, in the context of this experience, whether service and altruism can in fact empower women.

Again, it is not the purpose of this book to focus on why women's experience is different from what has been "normative" human experience. Nancy Chodorow and Carol Gilligan[3] (whose work shall inform this chapter) begin from the observation that girls are raised by women and thus identify with their primary caregiver, whereas boys more naturally

75

distinguish themselves from their mothers.[4] As Charlene Spretnak has noted,[5] there are those who claim biological foundations for these differences. However, whatever the cause of women's different experience, this chapter seeks to understand that experience and the effect a call to service and altruism would have on that experience.

Just what, then, is women's experience of self? In order to pursue this question, we shall explore Carol Gilligan's In a Different Voice, which is a study of the way in which women's sense of identity and ethical orientation develop. Gilligan's study is primarily about women's moral development. Her argument is that women, who have been considered by "normative" standards to be weak in our moral development, do in fact develop morally. However, women follow a different trajectory so that when we speak on moral issues, we do so "in a different voice." Because this voice is "different," she argues, it has not been recognized as a moral voice at all. Working from women's experience of ourselves as continuous with others and our resulting concern for relationship, Gilligan argues that women's moral development centers on an ethic of care that, although different from the "normative" ethical concern, is no less an actual ethic. Gilligan's work is important for the purpose of this chapter because she reveals how women's moral development parallels women's development of our identity. The final stage of women's moral development, as Gilligan constructs it, is the stage when a woman is able to address ethical situations in her own voice, not one determined by others. Inasmuch as I argue that this stage marks the development of a woman's own "perspective" and center of being, the development that Gilligan traces out parallels the journey women make towards liberation. Thus her study of how women develop ethically can inform our search for how women journey to selfhood--a journey marked by a woman's ability to speak in her own voice.

Gilligan entitles her study "in a different voice" because she argues that human development is not expressed in any one voice. However, she also stresses that:

> The different voice I describe is characterized not by gender but theme. Its association with women is an empirical

observation and it is primarily through women's voices that I trace its development. But this association is not absolute, and the contrasts between male and female voices are presented here to highlight a distinction between two modes of thought and to focus a problem of interpretation rather than to represent a generalization about either sex. [6]

Similarly, the use of "women" in this chapter is not meant to generalize about all women. It is used rather as a descriptive term for the experience of many women within this culture. Its use does not mean to suggest that all women share these experiences--nor does it preclude the possibility that some men may have similar experiences.

Then just what is women's experience of self? Nancy Chodorow has established first of all that women's experience is one of continuity and natural empathy with others. Women tend to feel others' feelings as our own. Carol Gilligan, drawing on the work of Chodorow, notes that this sense of continuity with others, which is central to women's experience, leads to a basic difficulty for women in the process of individuation--of separating ourselves from others. [7] A woman knows herself as intimately connected to others. This means, Gilligan notes, that for women "intimacy goes along with identity. . . ."[8] Our relationships to others are central to our experience of who we are. A woman "comes to know herself as she is known, through her relationships with others."[9] The fact that intimacy goes along with identity for women is juxtaposed by Gilligan with the "normative"--meaning male--experience that identity precedes intimacy. For the male once identity is established, connection and intimacy follow, although Gilligan argues that these remain problematic. For a woman, connectivity is a given, and "separation" and speaking in her own voice are problematic. [10]

A woman's experience of "knowing herself as she is known" is reflected in what Gilligan suggests to be a woman's concern for relationships. A woman, she argues, knows herself through relationships and her primary concern is to maintain those relationships. This sense of selfhood in continuity with others is revealed in a woman's moral development, which,

Gilligan argues, focuses around an "ethic of care"--the concern that no one be hurt, that relationships be kept intact. Describing a young girl's world, Gilligan says it "is a world of relationships and psychological truths where an awareness of the connection between people gives rise to a recognition of responsibility for one another, a perception of the need for response."[11] The fact that women are concerned with being responsible--being responsive to the needs of others--means that "women not only define themselves in a context of human relationship but also judge themselves in terms of their ability to care."[12] This is reflected in Gilligan's study in the way a young girl "locates herself in relation to the world, describing herself through actions that bring her into connection with others, elaborating ties through her ability to provide help."[13] A woman's sense of identity and self-worth are tied to "an ideal of care, against which she measures the worth of her activity."[14] Tied to an ideal of care that means sustaining and "elaborating" relationships, her sense of who she is and her self-worth are rooted in the way in which she responds to others. The young girl "sees a world of care and protection, a life lived with others whom 'you may love as much or even more than you love yourself.'"[15] Thus, Gilligan reveals, a woman's sense of self is tied to her notion of responsibility, which means "doing what others are counting on her to do regardless of what she herself wants."[16] This overriding concern with relationships and responsibilities is reflected in a "sensitivity to the needs of others and the assumption of responsibility for taking care" that lead women "to attend to voices other than their own. . . ."[17]

Gilligan's argument that women are concerned with caring for relationship is in many ways similar to de Beauvoir's observation that women are raised to please others. But whereas de Beauvoir reveals that pleasing others reinforces women's role as object, Gilligan argues that caring for others reflects a concern for others and is in fact ethical activity. She thus argues that women's concern for relationality is a strength, although a different kind of strength than the type normally thought of from male experience. Unfortunately, this concern for relationships often leads to a submergence of self in which a woman runs the danger of losing what

78

de Beauvoir calls her subjectivity as she seeks to meet others' needs. Hence this strength also can be dangerous, leading to the need to please others that de Beauvoir saw as so problematic.

This concern to "attend to voices other than their own" leads to a basic conflict for women. Attending to those voices, concerned to respond to another's needs, committed to the care and nurture of relationships, women understand our moral obligation to "avoid hurt"--to avoid damaging relationships through non-response to a need. Thus Gilligan observes, women tend to talk in a language that opposes "selfishness" or concern for ourselves and "responsibility" or responsiveness to others.[18] To be a responsible person comes to mean to attend to another's voice "regardless of what she herself wants." To attend to her own voice is thus by definition irresponsible to others and selfish. Thus, Gilligan affirms, a young girl experiences confusion as she reaches adolescence "as the 'I' who spoke clearly at eleven becomes in adolescence 'confused,' . . ."[19]

This confusion, I would suggest, reflects a young woman's loss of centeredness. No longer certain how to deal with her own thoughts and needs, afraid of being selfish, she becomes confused. And in the confusion, her "I," her centered self, is lost. Charting women's development in our present patriarchal society, Gilligan concludes that it is at adolescence, at the point of transition into adulthood, that women experience confusion over who we are. This confusion, which emerges from the tension between being attentive to herself and being attentive to others, results, as Gilligan describes it, in the submergence of the "I" and the attentiveness to filling the needs and expectations of others. As Gilligan shows, "the secrets of the female adolescent pertain to the silencing of her own voice, a silencing enforced by the wish not to hurt others. . . ."[20] This silence marks the "disappearance of the female self in adolescence by mapping an underground world kept secret because it is branded by others as selfish and wrong."[21] Afraid of being selfish, afraid of hearing her own voice and attending to her own needs, a young girl, Gilligan reveals, learns to stifle herself and seek her self-esteem through attention to the connections that are such a major part of her life.[22]

The submergence of a woman's self--the silencing
of her own voice in order to be attentive to the
voices of others--is, I would suggest, encouraged by
patriarchal society in several ways. First of all,
women's fear that attendance to our own voices will
"selfishly" isolate us from others and from an
essential part of ourselves is grounded in the very
real observation that what has been considered the
"normative" progression in the development of the
human self, as the self is understood in our
patriarchal society, has entailed a stage of
separation that has resulted in the severing of
relationships. Gilligan points out that Erik Erikson
in his understanding of "human" development, places
the primary emphasis in "normal" human development
upon separation. Separation, she notes, should lead
in Erikson's schema to intimacy and connectedness
(which can then progress to true human generativity,
creativity). But, she charges, in Erikson's life
cycle (which Gilligan suggests is really a "male life
cycle"),

> . . . there is little preparation [beyond
> an earlier stage of trust versus mistrust]
> for the intimacy of the first adult state.
> . . . The rest is separateness, with the
> result that development itself comes to be
> identified with separation and attachments
> appear to be impediments. . . .[23]

Although this passage in Gilligan focuses on Erikson,
her charge of the centrality of separation is made
more generally against others in the field of human
development as well.

Attachments and connections impede separation
and thus retard the development of the self. Women,
however, value relationships and judge ourselves by
our ability to care. Thus, when becoming a self,
being attentive to one's own voice, is understood as
becoming separate, as it is in our patriarchal
society, then women's fear that selfhood is selfish
is confirmed. Attendance to our own voices would
entail the very selfishness and irresponsibility we
fear.

As long as "selfhood" is thought of in this
"separate" manner, moreover, where attachments are
impediments, women's liberation to selfhood would
appear to threaten connections of all kinds. Since

women as relational have been the ones who keep society connected, our liberation thus threatens the whole society. Whereas feminists would affirm that women's liberation is a threat to patriarchal society, they would argue however that, inasmuch as the freedom they affirm is contextual, the selfhood they affirm is also contextual and thus affirms society. But in order to make this affirmation, feminists have had to envision a "new" way for people to understand themselves as selves in relation to others--a new way that does not so neatly oppose concern for self and concern for others. A new way that means that when women express our freedom by becoming selves in the midst of relationships, we reweave rather than sever the relationships so that different configurations of relationality result.

The submergence/silencing of women's self is further enhanced by women's fear that a "self," by its very nature, is aggressive and thus further threatens relationality. In Freud's theory of "normative" human development, Gilligan notes, the self develops through a "search for autonomy" which Freud describes as "the wish to gain control over the sources and objects of pleasure. . . ."[24] Freud, according to Gilligan, locates the beginning of this "search for autonomy" in the moment of an infant's initial screaming for help in "frustration when external sources evade"[25] it. The self, as described by Freud, created from "a primary separation, arising from disappointment and fueled by rage" is naturally aggressive and "assertion, linked to aggression, becomes the basis for relationships."[26] And relationships between naturally aggressive selves are potentially "explosive."[27] (Although women also would experience this initial frustration, works such as Chodorow's and Gilligan's that stress women's relationality and difficulty with separation would suggest that women's primary experience is not one of separation but of identity and connectedness and thus would modify the assumption that relationships are "naturally" tinged with aggression.) Thus women have good reason to fear that attendance to our own voices and the development of our own selfhood would lead to a potentially "explosive" aggression that would threaten the relationships so central to women's sense of identity. Thus Gilligan notes, "illuminating life as a web . . . women portray autonomy rather than attachment as the illusory and

81

dangerous quest."[28]

But Gilligan points out that Freud did note a
seeming exception to his assumption that humans are
naturally aggressive and that all human relationships
are tinged with aggression, namely that   .

> . . . the "single exception" to the
> "primary mutual hostility of human beings,"
> to the "aggressiveness" that "forms the
> basis of every relation of affection and
> love among people," . . . is located in
> women's experience, in "the mother's
> relation to her male child."[29]

Jean Baker Miller notes similarly that the theory
"that 'mankind' is basically self-seeking,
competitive, aggressive, and destructive. . . .
overlooks the fact that millions of people (most of
them women) have spent millions of hours for hundreds
of years giving their utmost to millions of
others."[30] Thus Miller argues that if theorists
would begin from women's experience the notion of
human nature would have to change--that as women
become selves in our own way aggression might not be
a natural "given."

The silencing of women into our state of
submerged selfhood is further enhanced by our
intuition that self-worth is tied to our responsible
caring for others. When our own voices appear to
threaten those relationships--when attendance to our
own voices would rearrange relationships to make room
for ourselves, and thus cause the "hurt" of adjusting
to change--then speaking in our own voices seem
selfish and irresponsible. Then, Gilligan observes,
women begin to distrust our voices and become
uncertain about our own worth apart from our ability
to care for others. Moreover this distrust and
uncertainty is fueled by a culture that devalues
women's voices as well. As Gilligan notes, a young
girl's voice is silenced not only because she fears
being selfish, but also because she fears that, "in
speaking, her voice will not be heard."[31] Jean
Baker Miller argues that women's self esteem is
lowered as well by a society that "deems women's
areas less valuable. . . ."[32] Thus even in
expressing our caring for the needs of others, a task
for which we are judged, women's voices are not
heard. (And if one is not heard by others, why

bother to speak, even to oneself?)

This inability to trust and hear our own voices is further enhanced by "the conventional feminine voice" which emerges "defining the self and proclaiming its worth on the basis of the ability to care for and protect others."[33] This "conventional feminine voice" is more than a woman's own central intuition that she should care for others. It is the voice of a society that declares that women should ultimately be "good" and judges women accordingly. This is the voice of "femininity" that equates goodness with self-sacrifice, that calls a woman to accept her place in man's life cycle, which has been that of "nurturer, caretaker, and helpmate, the weaver of . . . relationships. . . ."[34] A woman, according to the conventional feminine voice, is to be attentive to others, to neglect herself, so that society can be held together. This feminine voice calls a woman to goodness and enhances her distrust of her own voice by charging that any attention to herself is selfishness. This "conventional feminine voice" is, I would argue, the voice of patriarchal convention that often speaks in the voices of other women.

The belief that a woman's worth is in her goodness, defined as attendance to others through self-sacrifice, has kept, and continues to keep, women from our liberation. As Gilligan argues, this "notion that virtue for women lies in self-sacrifice has complicated the course of women's development by pitting the moral issue of goodness against the adult questions of responsibility and choice."[35] Moreover, I would suggest that the notion of self-sacrifice has done more than "complicate" women's lives--it has destroyed many of them. Elizabeth Cady Stanton once declared, "the thing which most retards and militates against women's self-development is self-sacrifice."[36] The "early proponents of women's rights," Gilligan notes, "equated self-sacrifice with slavery. . . ."[37] These women realized that the affirmation of "feminine virtue" as an "ideal of perfect devotion and self-abnegation" encouraged women not only to negate themselves, but also to devote themselves "not only to God but to men. . . ."[38] Thus self-sacrifice, the "theme song" of the conventional feminine voice, serves to reinforce the very structure of patriarchy from which women need to be freed. Modern feminists argue as well against the 'virtue of self-sacrifice" for women.[39] As Judith Plaskow states: "the language of self-sacrifice conflicts with personhood and becomes destructive when it suggests that the struggle to become a centered self to achieve fully independent selfhood is sinful."[40] She continues, a theology that calls self-sacrifice virtue "is not irrelevant to women's situation but rather serves to reinforce women's servitude."[41]

Thus we have seen that a woman's silencing/submergence of herself--which occurs through confusion created by the tension between attentiveness to her own voice and attentiveness to the voices of others--is reinforced by the patriarchal society in which she lives. The submergence of a woman's self should end developmentally, Gilligan notes however, with the woman's discovery that "the inclusion of herself in an expanding network of connections"[42] is necessary. But to do this, she must discover "a way of being with others that allows her to be with herself."[43] She needs to explore beyond the patriarchal definitions that confine her in a submerged and silent state, that place attentiveness to self and others in opposition, to "the discovery that responsiveness to self and responsiveness to others are connected rather than opposed."[44] She needs thus to move beyond patriarchal relationality as defined by "self-sacrifice" to a relationality that affirms the importance of being a self in-the-midst-of relationality. Thus, the transition from submerged/silent self to self-in-the-midst-of relationality which Gilligan describes in her theory of women's moral development as a developmental transition, I argue is the same movement that was described in Chapter I as the journey towards liberation. Just as Gilligan observes that women "develop" maturity by moving beyond an ethic of care described as self-sacrificial and beyond the notion that a woman's worth is judged by her "goodness," so women's liberation is a move beyond personhood defined by patriarchal relationality to a selfhood that affirms the self which, though in-the-midst-of relationality, is important for more than that relationality. As Mary Daly says, the journey to liberation is one where a woman "because she has a strong sense of her own worth . . . has the courage to accept her Self as not self-sacrificing."[45]

Mary Daly has said that women's journey to liberation begins with "a realization that there is an existential conflict between the self and structures that have given such crippling security."[46] In a similar fashion Carol Gilligan argues that the transition from submerged/silent self to a self that speaks in her own voice is initiated by a woman's awareness that "when only others are legitimized as the recipients of the woman's care, the exclusion of herself gives rise to problems in relationship, creating a disequilibrium. . . ."[47] Thus, Gilligan notes that a woman's transition from silence to hearing and speaking "centers on her struggle to disentangle her voice from the voices of others and to find a language that represents her experience of relationships and her sense of self."[48] As she disentangles her voice from the voices of others, as she begins to hear her own voice, a woman begins to "find her own language"--to speak in her own voice.

For Gilligan, the transition to full selfhood for women begins with our awareness that there are problems in relationships due to the disequilibrium that arises when we are inattentive to ourselves. One aspect of the "disequilibrium" women experience in this sort of relationship is revealed in the story of The Giving Tree[49]--a story described on its book jacket as "a tender story . . . a moving parable for readers of all ages." It is a story about the "conventional feminine" understanding of goodness as care for others "regardless" of what a woman herself wants. Yet in its portrayal of the "tenderness" of the giving tree, we can see the "disequilibrium" entailed in a woman's attentiveness to others with disregard for herself.

The Giving Tree is a story of a tree--a tree referred to as she--who lives solely in attentiveness to the needs of a little boy. Her joy in living lies not in the fullness of her limbs, the lusciousness of her fruit, the rich verdent greenness of her leaves--but only in filling the needs of the boy. Only when she pleases him is she happy. (The boy for his part, we should note, also seems to be concerned only for his own needs--and never for those of the tree.) At first, all the boy needs is a playmate--and this role the tree fulfills with great gladness, relishing their interaction. But then the boy becomes progressively more demanding. He needs money, so the tree gives him her leaves and fruit to sell. He needs a house, so the tree gives him her branches to build his house. He needs a boat to travel far away, so she gives him her trunk. And finally, he returns to her, a bent and aged and toothless old man, needing only a place to rest, and she offers him her self--her stump--as a seat. Her living in attentiveness to the boy has reduced her to a stump. Her care for the boy, her "goodness," her disregard for herself has resulted in her "stumpdom."

Throughout the story of the giving tree, the reader is told that the tree is happy. Although when the boy leaves her as a stump and travels far away, the author notes she is "not really" happy, upon his return she is happy once again for even a stump can be of use. The emphasis on the tree's happiness in her goodness reinforces the tree's self-sacrificial behavior (and the sacrificial behavior of women reading the story) and tends to blind the reader to the horror that the tree--which should have lived a productive life for several human generations--is, in the life span of one demanding boy, reduced to a stump, only a remnant of the tree she could have been. Mary Daly justifiably characterizes this story as "one of female rape and dismemberment."[50]

The Giving Tree reveals more than one aspect of the disequilibrium that results from one person's self-sacrificial behavior. The boy-man, who centers himself only on his own needs, is never truly happy. As an old man, he has no joy, no care for others, even for the tree. He is only weary. Dorothee Soelle describes the effect of self-sacrifice upon the one who demands it from another:

> . . . such a person destroys his own freedom. As the one in control he becomes the one controlled. In alienating others from what they wish to be and can become, he alienates himself. Because he concentrates on domination, on employing others as means to his own ends, he loses all other possibilities open to him. For example, he no longer pays attention to anything that does not fit his purpose. He loses the ability to enjoy living because he must constantly reinforce his life by accomplishments. The relationship between people is so interdependent that it is

impossible for one person to prosper at the expense of another. In the long run such exploitation proves detrimental to both.[51]

But there are other "problems in relationship" in addition to the ones revealed in The Giving Tree. Women's transition to speaking in our own voices, we have said, comes with the realization that there is a disequilibrium in relationships. This is the awareness that the total care of others without regard for ourselves leads not to happiness but to silencing, submerging, and "dismemberment." Feminine "goodness" encourages women to care for others with no one--not even ourselves--to care for us. As Jean Baker Miller notes, women, schooled in the myth of feminine goodness, cannot "tolerate or allow themselves to feel that their life activities are for themselves."[52] Thus she argues, "women feel compelled to find a way to translate their own motivations into a means of serving others and work at this all their lives."[53] That is, a woman's needs are not completely submerged, but cannot be attended to without "translation" into the language of serving others. This means, as Gilligan reveals, that women's silenced voices, our submerged selfhood, are not totally silenced and submerged but actually "surface" in the form of what she calls "indirect action." Women who live according to the convention of feminine goodness "claim to wish only to please. . . ."[54] But under the guise of pleasing others is hidden our real human need to have ourselves cared for as well. Gilligan notes, "in return for their goodness [women] expect to be loved and cared for."[55] Thus, concern for the well-being of others often masks a very real yet hidden dependency on the part of women. And feminine goodness or "service" may mask manipulative behavior that hides its own intentions under the guise of serving others. This "indirect action" leads thus to a basic dishonesty, for a woman in denying her own direct action, denies as well her own responsibility for what she does. Thus women hide our responsibility behind a mask of "innocence" and "altruism" that seeks only to please others and meet their needs. Through the language of service and altruism women may in fact be manipulating others to meet our own needs. The woman who lives according to feminine goodness--the "good woman"--thus "masks assertion in evasion, denying responsibility by claiming only to meet the needs of others. . . ."[56]

Women's growth toward maturity, Gilligan notes, comes with the awareness of our own "indirect action" and hidden dependencies. Because these indirect actions and dependencies are hidden behind the mask of feminine goodness, the transition to awareness is not a readily obvious one for women. In Gilligan's study the realization comes about through counseling. She tells for instance the story of a young woman undergoing abortion counseling. Through dialogue the woman was able to become aware of her own hidden, and thus unaccepted, responsibility for the unwanted pregnancy and was thus better able to make her own decision regarding an abortion. Choosing to see herself as innocent, the young woman was seeking an abortion as a "sacrifice, a submission to necessity. . . ."[57] She thus sought at first to avoid her own responsibility for the act. But through dialogue she came to realize that "her evasion of responsibility, critical to maintaining the innocence she considers necessary for self-respect, contradicts the reality of her participation in the abortion decision."[58] Once the "dishonesty in her plea of victimization"[59] was realized, she was able to begin to resolve the conflict in a direct way, consciously accepting her own participation and responsibility. Once her indirect action was discovered, she was able to begin to participate directly in the decision-making process.

Thus women's growth to maturity--and women's liberation--means not only the empowerment to speak in our own voices but also the act of taking responsibility for what we do. By masking responsibility behind "goodness" and innocence, altruism--caring for the voices of others regardless of her own--encourages a woman to evade her responsibility, and thus her own empowerment to direct action. Altruism and service keep women from making and claiming our own choices. And this effect is multiplied within a patriarchal society which in effect limits or denies women's choices. For "to the extent that women perceive themselves as having no choice, they correspondingly excuse themselves from the responsibility that decision entails."[60]

Altruism and service, in masking women's indirect action, mask our sin as well. The sin of hiding, as we have seen, is the sin of running from responsibility and hiding behind others who then make choices and determinations for you. Hiding and altruism, thus, appear to be the same activity for women. The conventions of feminine goodness encourage women in the sin of irresponsibility and hiding under the guise of being responsible (meaning responsive) to the needs of others. Under the mask of "responsibility" to the needs of others, which means responsiveness to others' needs, women evade our own real responsibility to create, name, and respond to the world from our own centers and in our own voices.

Altruism and service and an ethic of care that do not include the self among the others--among those who are cared for--may lead to "problems in relationship" not only through the dishonesty of indirect behavior that parades as innocence, but in the opposite way of direct behavior that severs relationships. When the attention to one's own voice is termed selfish and placed in opposition to an altruistic concern for the needs of others, then a woman whose very survival is being threatened may choose to "survive" at the expense of relationships. When self and other are so neatly opposed, as they are according to the "conventions of feminine goodness," the options are to be "good" or "bad," to be attentive to others or to be attentive to herself. The "bad woman," Gilligan argues, "forgoes or renounces the commitments that bind her in self-deception and betrayal."[61] In order to survive, she sees no other alternative than to completely sever the ties. To be "good," thus, is to be dishonest (a paradox!) whereas to be "bad" is to sever the very relations that are part of a woman's being.

"Bad" is, of course, that patriarchal name for a woman who would be attentive to herself. In some ways the liberated woman is the "bad" woman as characterized by patriarchal society. She is seen as shattering relations that have bound her. But the liberated woman is interested more--at least from the perspective of the present feminist movement--in unravelling ties (and not necessarily in severing them), and then reweaving them in a new way. The feminist perspective in general refuses the either/or opposition of "good" and "bad" woman and affirms a different possibility--of a self that can be attentive to herself while remaining connected to others.[62] However, the process of liberation may lead a woman through periods when she must, for a time, live in the mode of "survival."

The transition from the silent/submerged self to the empowered responsible self, we have seen, is one that entails an awareness of the disequilibrium in relationships that results from a woman's silencing of herself. The transition entails as well, Gilligan argues, a transformation in the woman's concern for relationality, from a concern that centers on attentiveness to the needs of others to one that understands care to be universal--inclusive of the self. This entails as well a transformation in the way women understand the opposition between self and other. The period of transformation is marked by the discovery that the two can be reconciled.

Care comes to be "universal in its condemnation of exploitation and hurt,"[63] and a woman enters the transition, Gilligan says, when she can include herself in her understanding of who is to be cared for. This transition "evolves around a central insight, that self and other are interdependent."[64] "In this sequence, the fact of interconnection informs the central, recurring recognition that just as the incidence of violence is in the end destructive to all, so the activity of care enhances both others and self."[65] Moreover, causing hurt is no longer seen as simply equated with failing to meet others' needs. Needs and hurts are interlocked--part of the web of relationships that are central to reality. A woman thus enters this transition when she comes to the realization that sometimes "there is no way of acting that avoids hurt to others as well as to herself, and in this sense, no choice that is 'right.'"[66] Care for others and self are then not necessarily opposed; they are placed within a context that is understood as infinitely more complicated.

Moreover, in this transition, Gilligan argues, women realize that "responsiveness to self and responsiveness to others are connected rather than opposed."[67] Caught in a relationship that felt unsatisfactory to her, one of the young women in Gilligan's study tells, for example, that she felt "selfish" and "wrong" for feeling that way. Rather than care for herself by dealing directly with the young man and asserting her own need (an act Gilligan argues would have been one "not of aggression but rather of communication. . . ."[68]), she turned to a "sordid affair behind his back," which, she admitted, was "subconsciously calculated to hurt him."[69] By refusing to deal directly with her needs and dealing with them indirectly through the affair, she came to admit, she hurt both herself and the two men. Her failure to care for herself by not taking "responsibility for having him stop hurting me" rather than enhancing the relationship, "perpetuated a cycle of hurt."[70] By not caring for herself, she brought more and not less hurt upon others. By caring for herself, and informing the young man of her own needs, she could have "provided an opportunity for response,"[71] that could have healed the relationship. Thus, this woman's refusal to care for herself did not make greater connection possible--as the ethic of care defined by altruism and service has suggested to women--but in fact led to greater disruption of relationship and deeper hurt.

Failure to attend to her own needs can affect a woman's caring for others in another way as well. As Dorothee Soelle points out, a woman who "lives in opposition to her own wishes exhibits, whether she wants to or not, an existence that is permeated by restraint."[72] Given the inter-relationship between people, "the atmosphere which comes into being around persons who--even subconsciously--offer themselves sacrifically has an unavoidable stifling effect on those who take advantage of them."[73] Thus, not only are relationships threatened by an attitude of caring for others without regard for herself, but human spontaneity and creativity are stifled as well. And the willingness to act sacrificially "when it becomes a habitual virtue" is, Soelle argues, "destructive and deadly," leading to a "psychic masochism" that she warns "will one day manifest itself in sadism."[74] Self-denial does not lead to greater possibilities for human relationship but gives rise to inhumanity, perpetuating "a cycle from which there is no escape: there are inhuman relationships that are maintained only by means of superhuman sacrifices, which in turn give rise to new inhuman relationships."[75] As Beverly Wildung Harrison suggests, "nothing can be good for society that concretely negates people."[76]

To state the effect from a positive perspective, attendance to one's own needs, the nurturing of one's own self, can lead to even richer lives and richer relationships. Elisabeth Moltmann-Wendel tells of a

91

legend about a woman "who was ordered to jump over a stream, but who refused to do so because she feared her love would be left behind."[77] Instead, having crossed the stream "she found her love on the other side."[78] Interpreting the woman's crossing of the stream as her beginning to listen to her own voice, to care for her own needs, Moltmann-Wendel notes "the search for the self begins by freeing oneself from the attitude of sacrifice and by opening oneself to one's own true spontaneity."[79] Then, in hearing her own voice, a woman is able, as Gilligan has suggested, to speak in a new language, to create a new response. Moltmann-Wendel concludes:

> Willing sacrifice establishes no new relationships to people; it renews nothing, it only creates new dependencies. Only when we have given up the sacrificial attitude do we experience a new emotional relationship to people, things, and circumstances.[80]

A woman's understanding of the complexity of relationships and of the inadequacy of an ethic of care that means attending to other's voices regardless of her own, and her desire to include herself in the circle of those for whom she cares, leads, Gilligan argues, to a new notion of responsibility. No longer does responsibility mean simple responsiveness. "Responsibility, separated from self-sacrifice," Gilligan argues, "becomes tied instead to the understanding of the causes of suffering and the ability to anticipate which actions are likely to eventuate in hurt."[81] A woman moves beyond a concern to end suffering to an awareness of what the cause might be. Whereas concern to avoid hurt is still essential to this new sense of responsibility, concern for her own need no longer is seen as a necessary cause of hurt. Rather, assertion is seen, as Gilligan suggests, not as threatening relation but as sustaining communication--taking responsibility that the relationship does not lose its "equilibrium." Then, "when assertion no longer seems dangerous, the concept of relationships changes from a bond of continuing dependence to a dynamic of interdependence."[82] And "the notion of care expands from the paralyzing injunction not to hurt others to an injunction to act responsively toward self and others and thus to sustain connection."[83] The "real constant" in relating to others, a woman comes to know, "'is the process' of making decisions with care, on the basis of what you know, and taking responsibility for choice while seeing the possible legitimacy of other solutions."[84]

This transition to this new kind of responsibility Gilligan notes, "requires a new kind of judgment."[85] But I would argue that this new kind of judgment is more than a new kind. It is also a new locus of responsible judgment. In attending to the voices of others, women judge ourselves according to the notion of "goodness." Although we are said to "judge ourselves," the actual locus of this judgment is not in our own center, not within us, but on the periphery where we are judged by others. To be "good" is to meet another's needs, which means, I would argue, that one is good because someone tells you that you are good. A new kind of judgment that reflects an "awareness" of the cause of suffering rather than seeking merely to fill the needs of the sufferer, rather than respond to another's judgment of proper responsiveness, suggests that the locus of judgment becomes the woman's own center of awareness. Aware of the complexity of relationship and seeking to determine the cause of suffering, a woman begins to act with a new kind of responsibility toward the relationships she seeks to nurture.

The awareness of "problems in relationships that create a disequilibrium," as noted earlier, leads to an awareness of a woman's need to be attentive to her own voice as well as to the voices of others. Being attentive to her own voice, I would argue, is a turn inward, not only because that voice has been submerged, but because it is her own voice. Once this turning inward has happened, a "different perspective" develops. This is a different perspective because the locus of perception has changed. Attentive to her own voice, a woman no longer turns outward to judge and determine her own behavior. Rather, I would suggest, the "I" re-emerges as the new judge and determiner. A woman finds a new center, her own center, from which decisions are made and pronounced. A woman's own voice emerges.

Dorothee Soelle, retelling one of Bertold Brecht's Calendar Tales, reveals how this process appeared in one woman's life. The first seventy years of this woman's life, she describes, are spent

93

in a "sacrificial obedience" that exhausts her "in working for and serving other people."[86]

> Altruism--a life devoted to others--is demanded of her, and she offers it freely and without complaint. She meets all expectations placed on her. She is self-less . . . --a person who re-sponds to the specific requests of others, who re-acts to the specific actions of others, who has developed very little individuality, very little spontaneity.[87]

But, reaching a transition point in her life, she discovers suddenly

> . . . how little she has developed as an individual during the seventy years spent in tending the family and keeping house, and how many other possibilities there have always been, possibilities for happiness, for involvement in the world, for shaping life according to her own point of view.[88] (emphasis mine)

Soelle concludes: "If the theme of the first seventy years of her life has been sacrifice, obedience, and constraint, the new theme might be called spontaneity, subjectivity, or freedom."[89] Having developed "her own point of view," she has a center from which to be subject, to claim her freedom to name herself and to spontaneously participate in the opportunities of life.

Or, as Gilligan interprets another woman's experience, to be able to make a choice she had first to hear her own voice and to "separate her perception of herself from the perceptions of others. . . ."[90] To perceive herself through others' perceptions of her, I would argue, is to view herself from outside herself. "For a long time," she said, "I was seeing myself as other people wanted to see me."[91] Just as when one's goodness is judged solely by meeting the needs of others the perspective is one from the "periphery"--so to perceive one's self through others' perception, to see one's self reflected in others' eyes--is to perceive from the periphery as well. To be able to choose, she had "to see herself directly rather than in reflection through others' eyes."[92]

94

To see ourselves as a reflection in others' eyes is what women do when we seek to please others. As de Beauvoir reveals, we then become objects even in our own eyes and thus lose our subjectivity, our center of awareness and agency. I am suggesting here that the move to what Gilligan calls a new type of responsibility and judgment parallels the move de Beauvoir referred to as the movement toward liberation.

To see herself directly, to perceive things from a different perspective, is, I argue, to have a center from which to hear and see and thence to speak. This is a new kind of "judgment"--a judgment that is not determined by the "conventions of feminine goodness" because the criterion of caring has changed. It is a new kind of judgment because the judgment, in attentiveness to the woman's own voice and to her new awareness, is made from a new center.

The formation of this new center reflects as well a new notion of selfhood. This process of centering is not the same process as the self-centered one revealed, for example in the thought of Reinhold Niebuhr,[93] where the centering self fortifies itself behind walls built in its vicious circling around itself. It is not formed through the severing of relations--not forged through separation. Nor is it a static self. Because of its very relational nature, it is always re-forming, re-sorting, and re-integrating itself in relationship and in response to others. As Catherine Keller suggests, this is a new notion of selfhood that "may show itself to be a process of continual change, of 'self-centering' rather than clinging to an immobile center. To center oneself is not to huddle in the walled citadel."[94] As Gilligan has suggested, what is constant in a woman's development is the process--the centering, the activity of hearing all voices including her own, and then integrating them and responding with her own decision in her own voice. Thus, the freedom of the self to create itself--the centering process of "selving"--does not cut her off, but weaves her together in her own way. Hearing the melodies of the universe, she sings her own song.[95]

As a woman's locus of judgment changes, Gilligan suggests the criterion for that judgment "shifts from

95

goodness to truth when the morality of action is assessed not on the basis of its appearance in the eyes of others, but in terms of the realities of its intention and consequence."[96] This criterion of "truth" I would argue is the criterion of honesty by which a woman affirms that her intentions and needs are part of her decisions and consciously affirms them, taking responsibility for the results. In turning "inward and acknowledging the self," a woman accepts "responsibility for choice."[97] Moving from an assumed and dishonest innocence, a woman finds and affirms her own center, her inner locus of perception and judgment, her own integrity. Hearing her own voice, she can then hear and integrate others', still with the intimacy that has been part of her identity. But now she has a center, a breathing space, a "room of her own"[98] from which to both hear and speak in her own voice. From her own center she can then integrate herself and others in a way not possible from the periphery where attentiveness to others is a distraction and attentiveness to herself is selfish.

What is crucial about this transformative stage in a woman's development, as detailed by Carol Gilligan, is that she moves through the ethic of caring, never disavowing its correctness, but expanding it to include herself. In so doing she becomes able to "express a judgment" rather than reflect someone else's judgment--to exist at her center, not at the periphery. When responsibility is understood in its "conventional interpretation" and becomes "confused with a responsiveness to others" then the recognition, the hearing and knowing, of one's self is impeded.[99] Responsibility, meaning making responses from her own center and being responsible for them, moves a woman from confusion--the confusion in which her self, her voice is lost--to integrity--an integrity that untangles and reweaves the confusion of voices that form her reality.

The formation of women's identity/integrity as explored in this chapter through Gilligan's explanation of women's moral development reveals, I would suggest, that for women true human integrity, honesty, maturity, and liberation lie not through service and altruism--attendance to the voices of others, putting the needs of others and the community first--but through a threshhold beyond altruism.

96

Through this threshhold, caring is not denied.
Rather, it is expanded to include the self. It
becomes truly universal. This move, I have argued,
draws a woman to her centered selfhood, one that
through altruism and service alone would be lost on
the periphery. It is from this center of selfhood
that a woman is able to speak in her own voice.

The notions of altruism and service thus, I
would argue, are not empowering to women. Rather,
they effectively block women from full
development--from human liberation. Service and
altruism look very much like the "convention of
feminine goodness" from which women are seeking
liberation. Thus, I would argue that the theological
symbols of altruism and service that are central
characteristics of the Christian community, while
affirming women's central understanding that care for
others is crucial to being human, are in effect
harmful to women. We have seen in this chapter that
in women's experience attendance to other's voices
precedes hearing our own voice and speaking in it.
Thus altruism and service mean to women, whose selves
have been submerged and silenced, not liberation but
self-sacrifice. Altruism and service keep women from
hearing our own voices and thus from centering to our
own human perspective. Moreover, we have seen that
the language of service and altruism can conceal a
basic dishonesty that blunts a woman's perception of
her own agency and responsibility. From women's
experience, the more empowering and liberating notion
is that of a call to self-centered self-hood, to a
new responsibility that, in awareness of the
complexity of interrelationships and in commitment to
the continuance of relationality, calls women to
speak in our own voices.

Women who live according to the conventions of
altruism and service and who effectively see the self
and others in opposition, Gilligan reveals, use "the
image of drifting along or riding it out" often to
describe "a life lived in response, guided by the
perception of others' needs. . . ."[100] They "see
no way of exercising control," of taking
charge/responsibility for their lives.[101] A woman
who finds empowerment to take responsibility, who is
liberated to hear her own voice and name herself,
exchanges the vision of innocence attained by a
denial of self--an innocence that is dishonest--for
an integrity that means taking control of, and

97

responsibility for, her own life.

Thus we must turn the question back to Christianity. Altruism and service, putting the needs of others and the community first, we have seen, do not lead contemporary women to be liberated from patriarchal systems. On the contrary they reinforce that system and women's place within it. Rather than liberate women to speak in our own voices, altruism and service effectively call women to sacrifice, or never to give birth to, ourselves. Thus we must ask again if Christianity, which Ruether and Schüssler-Fiorenza have argued can be a force for women's liberation today, can empower women to speak in our own voices. Can Christianity mean to women not the reinforcement of old patterns of submission and submergence that lead to a fundamental dishonesty, but rather a call to make choices, be responsible, and speak from our own centers? Can Christianity, that is, be characterized by theological symbols other than altruism and service that we have seen are not liberating possibilities for women today?

NOTES

[1] See Chapter I, pp. 10-12.

[2] See Chapter I, p. 11.

[3] Carol Gilligan, In a Different Voice: Psychological Theory and Women's Development (Cambridge, MA: Harvard University Press, 1982).

[4] Dorothy Dinnerstein, The Mermaid and the Minotaur: Sexual Arrangements and Human Malaise (New York: Harper & Row, 1976) works from this observation as well.

[5] See Charlene Spretnak's "Introduction" to The Politics of Women's Spirituality: Essays on the Rise of Spiritual Power Within the Feminist Movement (Garden City: Anchor Press/Doubleday, 1982) ed. Charlene Spretnak.

[6] Gilligan, p. 2.

[7] Ibid., p. 8.

[8] Ibid., p. 12.

[9] Ibid., p. 12.

[10] Whereas de Beauvoir bemoaned the fact that women are named according to our relationships, Gilligan works from the given fact that relationships are an important part of who women are. The maturation process she describes, which, I argue, parallels the liberation process described in Chapter I, is one of a woman's emerging as a self in the midst of connections. Others such as Catherine Keller argue for the importance of relationship in women's experience of who we are. Thus, the self that emerges into an "autonomy" in the midst of relationships (rather than a self whose autonomy is gained through the severing of relation) is seen as a more healthy way of being a full human self in the world, both for the "self" and for the world. See Catherine Keller, "From a Broken Web: Sexism, Separation, and Self" (Ph.D. dissertation, Claremont Graduate School, 1984). Now published as From a Broken Web: Separation, Sexism, and Self (Boston: Beacon Press, 1986).

[11]Gilligan, p. 30.

[12]Ibid., p. 17.

[13]Ibid., p. 35.

[14]Ibid., p. 35.

[15]Ibid., p. 38

[16]Ibid., p. 38.

[17]Ibid., p. 16.

[18]Ibid., p. 73.

[19]Ibid., p. 61.

[20]Ibid., p. 51.

[21]Ibid., p. 51.

[22]Jean Baker Miller notes "One central feature is that women stay with, build on, and develop in a context of attachment and affiliation with others. Indeed, women's sense of self becomes very much organized around being able to make and then to maintain affiliations and relationships." Jean Baker Miller, Toward a New Psychology of Women (Boston: Beacon Press, 1976), p. 83.

[23]Gilligan, pp. 12-13.

[24]Ibid., p. 46.

[25]Ibid., p. 46.

[26]Ibid., p. 46. For a study of how this initial rage, focused at the first care giver who failed to meet the immediate need of the infant, the mother, has led to rage against women and a sexist culture, see Dorothy Dinnerstein's The Mermaid and the Minotaur.

[27]Gilligan, p. 46.

[28]Ibid., p. 48.

[29]Ibid., p. 46.

[30]Miller, p. 69.

[31]Gilligan, p. 51.

[32]Miller, p. 75.

[33]Gilligan, p. 79.

[34]Ibid., p. 17.

[35]Ibid., p. 132.

[36]Quoted in Gilligan, p. 129.

[37]Ibid., p. 129.

[38]Ibid., p. 129.

[39]For example see Mary Daly, Gyn/Ecology: The Metaethics of Radical Feminism (Boston: Beacon Press, 1978), pp. 377-78, and Susan Dunfee, "The Sin of Hiding: A Feminist Critique of Reinhold Niebuhr's Account of the Sin of Pride," Soundings 65 (Fall 1982): 316-27.

[40]Judith Plaskow, Sex, Sin and Grace: Women's Experience and the Theologies of Reinhold Niebuhr and Paul Tillich (Washington, DC: University Press of America, 1980), p. 87.

[41]Ibid., p. 87. For a study of how women argue against self-sacrifice as an interpretation of the theological category of agape see Barbara Andolsen, "Agape in Feminist Ethics," Journal of Religious Ethics 9 (Spring 1981): 69-83.

[42]Gilligan, p. 39.

[43]Ibid., p. 53.

[44]Ibid., p. 61.

[45]Daly, Gyn/Ecology, p. 378.

[46]See Chapter I, p. 20.

[47]Gilligan, p. 74.

[48]Ibid., p. 51.

[49]Shel Silverstein, The Giving Tree (New York: Harper & Row, 1964).

[50]Daly, Gyn/Ecology, p. 90.

[51]Dorothee Soelle, Beyond Mere Obedience (New York: The Pilgrim Press, 1982), p. 35.

[52]Miller, p. 62.

[53]Ibid., p. 63.

[54]Gilligan, p. 67.

[55]Ibid., p. 67.

[56]Ibid., p. 71.

[57]Ibid., p. 86.

[58]Ibid., p. 86.

[59]Ibid., p. 86.

[60]Ibid., p. 67.

[61]Ibid., p. 71.

[62]See Anne Wilson Schaef, Women's Reality (Minneapolis: Winston Press, 1981) for a discussion of women having a relationship with themselves; and Catherine Keller for an ontology of the relational self.

[63]Gilligan, p. 74.

[64]Ibid., p. 74.

[65]Ibid., p. 74.

[66]Ibid., p. 118.

[67]Ibid., p. 61.

[68]Ibid., p. 61.

[69]Ibid., p. 60.

[70]Ibid., p. 61.

[71]Ibid., p. 61.

[72]Soelle, p. 37.

[73]Ibid., p. 37.

[74]Ibid., p. 37.

[75]Ibid., p. 38.

[76]Beverly Wildung Harrison, Our Right to Choose: Toward a New Ethic of Abortion (Boston: Beacon Press, 1983), p. 48.

[77]Elisabeth Moltmann-Wendel, Liberty, Equality, Sisterhood (Philadelphia: Fortress Press, 1978), p. 80.

[78]Ibid., p. 80.

[79]Ibid., p. 80.

[80]Ibid., p. 80.

[81]Gilligan, p. 134 (emphasis mine).

[82]Ibid., p. 149.

[83]Ibid., p. 149.

[84]Ibid., p. 148.

[85]Ibid., p. 82-83.

[86]Soelle, p. 31.

[87]Ibid., p. 31.

[88]Ibid., p. 32.

[89]Ibid., p. 33.

[90]Gilligan, p. 52.

[91]Ibid., p. 52.

[92]Ibid., p. 52.

[93]See Chapter I, pp. 18-20.

103

[94]Keller, p. 67.

[95]For a poignant story of a woman who never could bring herself to cut through the conventions of feminine goodness to sing her own song, see Gloria Steinem's story of her mother, "Ruth's Song (Because She Could Not Sing It)" in Outrageous Acts and Everyday Rebellions (New York: Holt, Rinehart and Winston, 1983).

[96]Gilligan, p. 83.

[97]Ibid., p. 85.

[98]Virginia Woolf, A Room of One's Own (New York: Harcourt Brace Jovanovich, 1957).

[99]Gilligan, p. 127.

[100]Ibid., p. 143.

[101]Ibid., p. 143.

CHAPTER IV

Self-Sacrifice Revisited

We have seen in Chapter III that the theological symbols of service and altruism--of putting the needs of others and the community first--are not liberating or empowering for women today. From the perspective of contemporary women's experience we have seen that altruism and service reinforce women's more natural tendency to consider "other voices" than our own and discourage the development of our own perspective, our own center of judgment, our own voice. Thus, through the call to service and altruism, women are encouraged to live solely for others and according to the patriarchal convention of feminine goodness, to silence our own voices and deny our own responsibility in a responsiveness to others that reinforces not liberation but servility. Far from calling women to responsible selfhood, service and altruism mean for women the negation of selfhood.

Yet if we consider again the claim of Elisabeth Schüssler-Fiorenza, Rosemary Ruether, and others that Christianity can be liberating for women today, we remember that the early non-patriarchal alternative Christian community that Schüssler-Fiorenza has reconstructed (whose history she argues can be a symbol for women's empowerment today)--one which was characterized by service and altruism--was not one noted for its servility. That is, its service and altruism did not necessarily entail servility. Rather, to a dominant patriarchal society that lived off of the servility of others, this alternative Christian community offered "offense." It was the "gradually patriarchalized" Christian community that sought not to offend the dominant patriarchal culture that reinforced structures of subordination and servility. The offense created by the alternative community suggests, rather, that its altruism and service did not mean service to the patriarchal culture--but something else. And indeed, if we follow the argument of Schüssler-Fiorenza, the early Christian community that she reconstructs came into conflict with the dominant patriarchal culture precisely because it refused to appropriate patriarchal patterns of domination and submissiveness. The followers of Jesus were a community of equals where all served and none were servile. And in this community, Schüssler-Fiorenza argues, the disenfranchised found liberation and self-esteem and positions of leadership and responsibility. This community--this liberation community--then was characterized not only by service and altruism but by the empowerment of people to be free to preach and teach and speak in their own voices.

It would appear then that the experience of the Christian community is not about servility and the loss of selfhood but about the empowerment of the subordinated to become persons. Yet we have seen that the theological symbols of altruism and service do not mean to women the empowerment to become persons. Rather, service and altruism mean for women the negation of our selfhood. Thus we are left with a dilemma. If the Christian community is truly about empowerment, especially the empowerment of the marginalized, then we must ask whether this community is adequately characterized by a service and altruism that do not lead to such empowerment for women--or whether there might be a better way--other theological symbols--to characterize the Christian community that can be both true to the Christian experience and yet empowering to women.

In Chapter V we shall explore the possibility of other theological symbols to characterize the Christian experience. However, before making this methodological move, I would suggest that we not abandon the notions of service and altruism immediately but explore more fully what Christianity means by service and altruism as they impact people's lives. Although we have seen that service and altruism mean self-sacrifice--the negation of the self--for women, I would argue that it is not necessarily correct to assume that service and altruism have been understood by the Christian tradition to mean the negation of the self. Thus I propose to explore more fully the theological symbols of service and altruism, putting the needs of others and the community first, to see if they necessarily entail the negation and sacrifice of the self that we have seen they mean for women in our experience of selfhood.

Although we could approach this task in a variety of ways, I will begin this chapter with a discussion of the work of Reinhold Niebuhr. Niebuhr, I would argue, is useful for the purpose of this chapter because he describes the Christian experience both as one in which a person "lives in and for others, in the general orientation of loyalty to and love of God"[1]--or altruism and service as we have been calling it--and as self-sacrificial. He thus makes the connection that a life of service and altruism means self-sacrifice--which we have argued from women's perspective is the case. Let us look first at Niebuhr's work to determine just what he means by self-sacrifice--to see if he means the negation of the self. Or--to ask the question in another way, to discern what self it is that Niebuhr argues is to be sacrificed in a life of service and altruism.

Turning to Niebuhr, then, I would argue as I suggested in Chapter I[2] that the self that Niebuhr says is sacrificed is the self-concerned self that turns inward on itself in a "vicious circle" making of itself a fortress or a walled city. That is, the self sacrificed is the self created through the sin of pride. Thus, the result of this sacrificial act would be not the negation of the self but its release from the bondage to pride to live a life in concern for relationship with others. Although Niebuhr uses the language of self-sacrifice to describe the Christian experience, the life of altruism and service he describes is not one of self-negation but of self-fulfillment as the self finds its true expression in a life lived in harmony with other lives.

Niebuhr, as we have seen, argues that humanity is both finite and free--subject to the "vicissitudes" of nature, yet in its freedom, able to transcend that nature.[3] True humanity exists, he argues, in the tension between the two poles. And the law of human nature, the law of true human fulfillment, is the "law of love." He argues, "the final law for man in his condition of finiteness and freedom" is the law of love because "man in his freedom is unable to make himself in his finiteness his own end."[4] Human transcendence, that is, leads persons to transcend even themselves in their finite narrowness. This capacity for self-transcendence thus opens persons up beyond themselves to live in loving relations with others. The human individual as transcendent is not meant to live alone--to be in him/herself. Rather, true human selfhood is revealed in the law of love which is the constant transcendent

107

opening up of the self to live vulnerably "in and for others."

However, Niebuhr argues, human sinfulness distorts the situation. Rather than live transcendently "in and for others," human beings turn their transcendence in on themselves. In "undue self-concern," human beings turn their freedom, which ultimately should be expressed "in and for others," toward themselves. Thus Niebuhr says, "human evil, primarily expressed in undue self-concern, is a corruption of its essential freedom and grows with its freedom."[5] Rather than spiraling from their center outward in greater circles of self-transcendence revealed in greater openness to others, persons turn the spiral into a vicious circle around themselves, closing themselves off from others.

Although the motion of transcendence is clearly an ascending one for Niebuhr--one from which the person gains a transcendent perspective even on her/himself--I interpret Niebuhr to mean that the motion of transcendence leads ultimately not vertically outside of history, but in a spiraling motion, back into history. Niebuhr argues that the transcendent self reaches its limit in a confrontation with God.[6] Human transcendence that has recognized its limitation is thus, I argue, redirected not upward but outward. The transcendent motion then becomes one of spiraling upward and outward, beyond the narrow self to live in relation to others.

Meant to transcend bonds of narrowness, humans use their trancendence to shut themselves in, closing themselves off, in a self-concerned vicious circling that creates towers of self-defense. Niebuhr teaches, in their towers of self-concern created out of circling about their own interest as if those were the only interests to be concerned about, persons think that they are free. But their sin has been a misuse of their freedom. Instead of living according to the true law of their nature, they live according to their sin, the misuse of their freedom. To use a Pauline phrase, they are in bondage--in bondage in a prison they have created out of their own freedom--in bondage to a self-concern that creates in them the need to defend themselves from within their towers. They are thus cut off from each other and from their true calling to live "in and for each other." Sin,

Niebuhr argues, "is occasioned precisely by the fact
that man refuses to admit his 'creatureliness' and to
acknowledge himself as merely a member of a total
unity of life."[7] In their sin, persons deny that
they are connected to others as members "of a total
unity of life" and seek to live instead as if they
were autonomous. And human relations are
characterized by a "will-to-power,"[8] as each
individual seeks to defend itself by acts of
aggression against others. Thus human sinfulness
results not only in human entrapment, but also in the
severing of human relations.

But the Christian experience, Niebuhr argues, is
one in which humanity is redeemed from its bondage.
The God of Christianity is one who shatters the
vicious circles in which humans are preoccupied with
themselves and the towers they have erected for their
own defense and calls persons to be born anew--to be
reborn into their full humanity. This new self,
judged and redeemed by God, "is more truly a real
self because the vicious circle of self-centeredness
has been broken."[9] Freed from its bondage, the
self is free to live according to the law of its
nature--to live "in and for others" that is, the life
of altruism and service.

Niebuhr thus reveals that through the experience
of shattering and crucifixion,[10] through the
sacrifice of the self, the real self emerges as one
able to live according to its calling. Thus, I would
suggest that, although Niebuhr uses the language of
crucifixion and sacrifice, the self is not truly
negated.[11] Rather, what is shattered and
sacrificed is the self created in human sinfulness.
The shattering is not a negation of the self. It
points instead to a transformation, a birthing
experience, in which the self is liberated from its
own confinement.[12] Thus I would argue that the
life of altruism and service that Niebuhr and
Schüssler-Fiorenza have said are the Christian
experience of a life liberated and lived to its
fullness, does not mean the sacrifice of selfhood.
Rather, altruism and service are expressions of a
true selfhood that lives in concern for others. They
are an affirmation that true human wholeness is lived
in openness and relationality and in concern for
others.

That service and altruism, what Niebuhr calls

the life lived according to the law of love, do not
entail self-sacrifice can be seen in the way he
characterizes the law of love in itself. Although
Niebuhr describes the self that lives according to
the law of love as self-sacrificial, when he
describes his vision of what this life lived
according to the law of love looks like, the self is
still readily evident. The law of love, Niebuhr
says, is characterized by three terms. Drawing from
Scripture, he argues that "Thou shalt love the Lord
thy God" means "the perfect relation of the soul to
God in which obedience is transcended by love, trust,
and confidence."[13] "With all thy heart and all thy
soul and all thy mind" he describes as "the perfect
internal harmony of the soul with itself in all of
its desires and impulses."[14] And, "thou shalt love
thy neighbor as thyself" he simply characterizes as
"the perfect harmony of life with life."[15] There
is no mention of self-sacrifice here--rather of a
harmony of lives. The self, I argue, is still
evident.

And indeed Niebuhr has argued that Christianity
is really about the creation of selfhood. He says:

> Christianity is responsible for a
> heightened sense of individuality because,
> according to the Christian faith, the human
> spirit in its freedom is finally bound only
> by the will of God, and the secret of its
> heart is only fully known and judged by the
> divine wisdom.[16]

Standing before the Christian God, known from beyond
themselves, Christians, Niebuhr argues, realize their
own individuality.

As he expands what this "harmony of life with
life" might mean, Niebuhr describes the relationship
between persons living according to the law of love
as a "relationship in which spirit meets spirit in a
dimension in which both the uniformities and the
differences of nature, which bind men together and
separate them, are transcended."[17] As he
reiterates what he has called the human problem, he
continues:

> This is no simple possibility. Each soul
> remains, in a sense, inscrutable to its
> fellows. . . . All human love between

110

person and person is frustrated by
inscrutable mysteries in the heart of each
person and by opaque "walls of partition"
between man and man.[18]

Human persons need to transcend these walls of
partition between them that make the longings of
one's heart an inscrutable mystery to another. But
this overcoming of walls is not a simple
possibility. Rather he says:

Inasfar as human love is a possibility, . .
. it is always partly a relation between
the soul and soul via their common relation
to God. . . . Where the love of God does
not undergird and complete the relation of
man to man, the differences which nature
creates and sin accentuates, differences of
geography, race, time, place and history,
separate men from one another.[19]

The problem Niebuhr experiences is that people
experience themselves as cut off from each other and
then in their sin erect barriers that cut them off
further from what should be their true state of
fulfillment, one of community, sharing and concern
for others. The law of love, then--the drive for a
harmonious unity between persons which is possible
only when walls, the opaque walls of partition that
hide them from each other, are transcended so that
true communion is possible--is only a possibility
when the love of God "undergirds and completes" the
relation.

    The law of love--the Christian experience of
liberation into true human fulfillment--is thus for
Niebuhr not necessarily the denial of self but the
transcending of the barriers that bind people within
themselves (barriers that I have suggested are the
result of what Niebuhr calls the sin of pride),
separating them off from one another, making
impossible the communion of soul with soul. Living
in and for others--what we have called service and
altruism--means for Niebuhr living in harmony beyond
the boundaries of premature prideful selfhood. It
leads to a self that must always be
self-shattering--and in this sense is
self-sacrificial. But, through this shattering
experience one does not lose selfhood, for it is not
the self but the prematurely bounded self that is

being shattered. Rather, through this shattering one finds the fulfillment of the intuition of what true human selfhood is all about: a harmony between beings who live in and for each other and realize that their true fulfillment lies not in separate selfhood, but in selfhood that is deeply interrelational.

Although I have used inclusive language to characterize Niebuhr's argument, Niebuhr's understanding of human nature and the human problem, as we have seen in Chapters I and III, is not in fact inclusive of women's experience. Rather, I would suggest, they reflect what Gilligan has shown to be the experience of males within this culture. Niebuhr has said that humans in their sin "naturally" close themselves off from each other. Rather than live "trancendently" in openness and harmony with others, they forge a separate selfhood cutting themselves off from others. They become autonomous--a law unto themselves. And they defend their "walledness" by an aggressiveness towards others. This reflects the development of selfhood in the male experience--a selfhood Gilligan has charged is characterized by separation and aggression, and a selfhood that Niebuhr terms sinful and problematic. True selfhood, Niebuhr argues, lies beyond separation; it lies in a life lived in openness to others. Niebuhr calls the life lived thus--the life of service and altruism--self-sacrificial, I would suggest, because the premature sinful self, which humanity naturally forms and which constantly closes in on itself, must be shattered and crucified--literally sacrificed. In a culture where selfhood is defined by that closed and separate selfhood, such a life would be experienced as self-sacrificial. Moreover, I would suggest that Niebuhr calls a life lived according to the law of love self-sacrificial because, given the claims and counter-claims of history, given the "natural" aggressiveness of human nature, those who refuse to be involved in building a defensive fortress in a world where selves are fortresses and relationality explosive would end up (and have ended up) on the "edge" of history. The term self-sacrifice is thus a descriptive term, pointing both to the shattering of "normative" sinful selfhood and to what happens when one lives a life of such total vulnerability.

In exploring the thought of Reinhold Niebuhr I

have thus argued that even though he uses the language of self-sacrifice to describe a life lived fully according to the law of love (service and altruism), selfhood is not negated. Rather, the self is _assumed_. The notions of service and altruism assume a self. Thus if altruism and service characterize the liberated Christian life, then I would argue _that_ life is one characterized by a self that lives openly with others with central concern for the enhancement of relationships. Because Niebuhr writes from an experience where the self is assumed, his emphasis in his description of the Christian experience is on service and altruism that reflect the transformation of that self from separation and cut-off-ness to relatedness. And because the assumed self that he writes about is one that lives "naturally" for itself (naturally uses its freedom for its own concerns), he characterizes the life of altruism and service as one _lived for others_. Thus we can argue that the Christian experience is both about living in harmonious relationship with others and about being a self that lives with others. The notions of service and altruism entail being a self that can live in relationships of harmony with others. Thus the affirmation that the Christian experience of liberation is one characterized by altruism and service does not contradict the assertion that Christianity is also about human empowerment to human selfhood. But, since it would seem that service and altruism best describe this experience of liberation to full selfhood when directed to people for whom the self is already experienced--is assumed--they do not adequately express or call into being the full Christian experience of liberation for all people. It would seem then that if Christianity is about empowerment, and if it is to be concerned with _women's_ empowerment, then it needs to express the experience of liberation (and the call to that liberation) in a way other than service and altruism.

However, although service and altruism do not adequately express to women's experience the affirmation or call to selfhood since the self is assumed and not called into being, they do reflect human empowerment in two ways. First of all, they reflect in _men's_ experience, according to Niebuhr's argument, a liberation from bondage and the empowerment to live their true selfhood. Liberated from living in concern solely for themselves and from being cut off from the relationality that undergirds all life, men are free to live lives connected to others. Secondly, the notion that full human selfhood is expressed in service and altruism is an affirmation to women's intuition that care and concern for relationships are central to human wholeness. Where male development in patriarchal culture means a separation and an aggression that make relationality problematic and dangerous, Christianity, as viewed through Niebuhr, and its affirmation of service and altruism affirms that true human fulfillment lies in a shattering of separation, the transcending of aggression, and a living in vulnerable relationality with others.

We have seen in Chapters I and III that women such as Jean Baker Miller (A New Psychology of Women), Carol Gilligan (In A Different Voice), and Anne Wilson Schaef (Women's Reality)[20] among others, are suggesting that women's experience of ourselves and our reality points to a different way of being a self and being in relation to the world. Where selfhood has been defined by "separation," a woman's concern for relationality has been devalued as "weakness," her "self" as "wishy-washy" and her moral development as immature. In these women's suggestions that women have a new psychology, a different voice and our own different reality, they are saying that women's weakness is not a weakness but another experience. From the perspective of this different experience, and in the context of the explosive potential that does accompany "separate" selves, these women are arguing that women's "weakness" is actually a strength. Reality and true humanity, they argue, are all about relationship. No one can and truly does exist by her/himself. Separation is an illusion, a lie. The hope for the future of the world, they insist, lies in this realization and the complementary affirmation that relationality and care for the webbedness of life are in fact the fullest expression of humanity.

Far from devaluing women's experience of relationality and caring as does the patriarchal culture, the Christian understanding that true humanity lies in a relationality--a relationality we have seen expressed in the terms altruism and service--affirms that very intuition. True humanity, Niebuhr has said, is experienced in the continual shattering of human pretensions to separation and

114

self-sufficiency. It involves a transcendence
reflected in a life of caring for the needs of
others. Thus, although the description of the
Christian experience of liberation as service and
altruism does not empower women to speak in our own
voices, it actually does affirm women's experience of
the importance of relationality and caring.[21]

Niebuhr, in his claim that altruism and
service--what he calls the law of love--mean
self-sacrifice, does not speak for all of Christian
tradition. And indeed I am not trying to argue here
that there has not been a major strain of Christian
tradition that has understood Christianity to be
about a non-dialectical sacrifice of the self.[22]
Niebuhr is used here as one who understood altruism
and service--life lived by the law of love--to be
self-sacrificial. And, I have argued that although
he uses the language of self-sacrifice, in fact, in
the expression of service and altruism, the self is
not negated at all.

Daniel Day Williams, a contemporary of Niebuhr,
argues with Niebuhr on the other hand, that the "law
of love"--what we have called service and altruism
and what Williams calls love or agape--does not mean
self-sacrifice. We can thus turn to Williams as an
example of one within the Christian tradition who
argues against the insistence that Christian love
means the sacrifice of the self. Williams argues,
that the vision of a community that knows the harmony
of life with life--the liberated Christian
community--does not entail the "negation of any self,
but rather the fulfillment of it"[23]--that agape
"intends a good which does include the ultimate good
of the self."[24] The real good, Williams notes,
"involves qualitative transformation of the order of
life into a more subtle and complete mutual
participation"[25] and is expressed in a "universal
community . . . in which each member is more free,
more mature, more powerful through what he gives to
and receives from every other member. . . ."[26]
This "order of mutuality" suggests that "all selves,
all real values have their place. While each gives
itself to the whole, each has its own claim upon the
whole. For the good is just the good of each in the
good of all."[27] Thus he conlcudes:

It is . . . not a denial of Christian love
to intend my own good in the service of the

Kingdom. That is the foundation of human
struggles for freedom, justice, adequate
material goods, more universal
brotherhood.[28]

Thus Williams argues that concern for the self--the
inclusion of the self in the ethic of caring--is "not
denied" by the Christian notion of love. Christians
realize that the struggle for freedom and justice are
in themselves an expression of "the Kingdom." The
good of the individual is a part of the good of the
all, and the good of the all involves the
"transformation of the order of life into a more
subtle and complete mutual participation." The "good
of the all" and the Kingdom include the freedom,
justice and selfhood of each individual. Thus,
Williams argues that the affirmation of selfhood is
"not denied" in the Christian notion of agape--what
we have called service and altruism. Rather--care is
mutual, universal. "There is a work of God,"
Williams says, "in the midst of this dark reality
which brings forth matured, self-reliant, free
persons. . . ."[29]

Thus in Williams we find a voice within
Christianity that affirms the importance of selfhood
and the need for each to be cared for . . . the
universality of the ethic of caring. We can find the
grounds within Christianity for the affirmation of
women's empowerment through the extension of the
ethic of caring to include the self. Moreover,
Williams has identified the development of "matured,
self-reliant, free persons" as the work of God . . .
as part of God's work for the development of the
Kingdom of God. Clearly then Williams' vision of
Christianity is one that would affirm the liberated
state to which women are arriving.

But whereas Williams affirms the importance of
the individual and of the development of "matured,
self-reliant, free persons," agape, service and
altruism, do not call that selfhood into being.
Rather, selfhood is "not denied" in agape. The call
to agape, that is, assumes a self that is not to be
denied. Working from an "assumed" self, Williams
argues that agape leads to a full humanity not
through a process of self negation, nor through a
shattering, but through transformative growth and
extension. The self is opened up to care for more
than itself and to include the good of the self

116

within the context of the good of the all. The self comes to live a life of connection and fluidity with others, and lives in a concern to enrich not only itself but those to whom it is connected. The fullness of life is realized to be a communal fullness, and the goal of life becomes the enhancement of that communal fullness (which means not only the fullness of the all, but of each, as well). He states:

> The love which is revealed in Christ is a love which seeks the fulfillment of all things in such a relationship to one another that what flows from the life of each enriches the life of all, and each participant in the whole life finds his own good realized through the giving of self to the life of the whole.
>
> . . . The fuller good resides where this life and that life, this natural fact and that spiritual aspiration go together in such a way that each person becomes a more whole person in serving the total order of life actual and possible of which he is a part.[30]

Where Niebuhr argued that the self had to be shattered and a new self born, Williams argues that the transformation to human fullness is an expansion of human selfhood--an organic growth--that constantly challenges the self to consider itself in an ever-enlarging, interlocking web of reality. Thus Williams argues that in love--in service and altruism--the self is not sacrificed but remains. Yet the ultimate good of the self, its fulfillment, is reached through "giving of self to the life of the whole" or what we have called service and altruism. The self is not lost, but is opened up to realize its connection to the world and thus is encouraged to expand its understanding of what is good for itself. It is transformed, enlarged, and seeks to serve "the total order of life actual and and possible of which [it] is a part."

Just as the self is not shattered but grows outward to its fulfillment so, for Williams, human loves are extended and expanded by God's love, which transforms them to seek not "possession" but "participation."[31] Such participation entails the willingness to be involved with the other and to risk accepting that other's freedom. It means making another's history one's own. It means encouraging another to freedom even at the risk of one's own existence.[32] The movement of <u>agape</u>--which is the expression of human liberation and fullness from the Christian perspective--as Williams describes it is one in which an assumed and affirmed self is opened up to an increasing involvement in and concern for the lives of others. The self's boundaries are not shattered but are expanded to include the history of another. Human growth moves toward greater intimacy toward another--a greater vulnerability and permeability which is "the capacity to be acted upon, to be moved by another. . . ."[33] One who is closed is opened up to be affected by another.

Williams thus argues that the human problem is that persons are closed and need to be acted upon; they are centered on their own history and need to be opened to risk making another's history their own. Full humanity is revealed in greater risks of greater intimacy, an intimacy that is willing to suffer for another's freedom. Thus, although Williams has suggested that the development of matured, self-reliant persons may be the work of God, the work of <u>agape</u> seems to be transforming those matured, self-reliant persons into loving persons whose selfhood is opened up to live in greater intimacy with others.

Although Williams "argues" with Niebuhr that the Christian experience of service and altruism is not one that should sacrifice or shatter the self but one that should stretch and open the self up, he reflects a position, for the purposes of this chapter, similar to that of Niebuhr. The self is affirmed and not negated, and there is a "work of God . . . which brings forth matured, self-reliant, free persons," but the work of Christian love--of service and altruism--is one that assumes the self rather than calls that self into being. <u>Agape</u> transforms a person's understanding of her/his selfhood from a narrow-closed sense grounded in the self's own needs to a larger interconnected matrix in which the other's needs--the other's history--becomes part of her/his own.

<u>Agape</u> thus is experienced by Williams as a transformation that means risking one's self by

118

involvement with others. It is an act in which the self risks greater vulnerability. I would argue that even for Williams, who argues that the self is not negated through love, service and altruism (although affirmed as universal and thus inclusive of the self) are not the source of the lover's selfhood. The call to service and altruism seems rather to be the call to be engaged in the lives of others. Whereas this would affirm the intuition that true humanity lies in being involved, in being engaged, and thus again affirms women's experience of the centrality of relatedness to life, the notion of agape means that an assumed selfhood is transformed through love to move beyond itself and does not appear to offer the grounds for the call to be a self-concerned, self-centered self--a call that would empower women to become "matured, self-reliant, free persons."

If the Christian notion of human liberation means, as I am suggesting, both the affirmation of selfhood and the intuition that true selfhood lies in being intimately concerned for relationships with others, then the notions of service and altruism can adequately describe human liberation and human wholeness only when the self is assumed. That is, they express human wholeness only from what we have been calling the male experience, one that assumes a self it knows to be too easily closed off from others. For this experience, service and altruism lead to a self in relation. But for women's experience, service and altruism do not mean human wholeness at all. Women who experience ourselves in relation need the call to self-centering to experience our human fullness, our liberation.

Paul Tillich in Love, Power and Justice[34] suggests similarly that the call to selfhood does not lie through the call to love--to service and altruism. Love alone, in fact, cannot assure selfhood. Rather, he argues that for love to be fulfilled it must include a power and justice that affirm the importance of the self-centered person who is doing the loving. Love, Tillich argues, "reunites that which is self-centered and individual."[35] For Tillich, self-centeredness is not a problem. Rather, Tillich argues, without "separation there is no love and no life."[36] Centeredness is crucial and is not shattered by an act of love. Rather, "the centre of a completely individualized being cannot be entered by any other individualized being. . . ."[37] Thus, the highest form of love, Tillich states, is one that "preserves the separation of the self-centered self, and nevertheless actualizes their reunion in love."[38] It "is the love which preserves the individual who is both the subject and the object of love."[39] Thus Tillich affirms that love means both the reunion, the intimacy, and the separation of self-centered selves.[40]

But, for Tillich, this act of love cannot exist by itself without being reduced to "chaotic self-surrender" in the destruction of the lover and the love.[41] Rather, love must include justice.

> It is justice to oneself to affirm one's own power of being and to accept the claim for justice which is implied in this power. Without this justice, there is no reuniting love, because there is nothing to unite.[42]

Love without justice would be chaos. But with a justice that affirms the separate self, the highest form of love is a possibility. Thus for Tillich, the "law of love," to use Niebuhr's expression for the experience of full humanity affirmed through Christianity, cannot be expressed without the affirmation of the self and its center of being. Love must be corrected by justice to be the reconciling of two separate beings. Love combined with justice as an expression of each person's power to be is a connection, an act of relationality, and an affirmation of self-centeredness. Thus, we can see Tillich argues that love presumes self-centeredness and that the call to self-centeredness is not reflected in the call to love. Rather, the call to centeredness (and the affirmation of that centeredness) is reflected in some other notion that calls the self to affirm its own power and accept its own claim to justice--to be considered within the circle of care.

I have argued in Chapter III that the notions of service and altruism--what Niebuhr says reflect the law of love--are not empowering to women. I have argued in this chapter that service and altruism do not fully express the vision of full humanity suggested in either the liberation of the early Christian community nor in the vision of the law of love of Niebuhr (or Williams or Tillich). Rather, a

more adequate expression of the vision of full
humanity would be one that includes both the notion
of caring expressed in the notions of service and
altruism and the call to a centered selfhood
expressed in the metaphor of speaking in one's own
voice. This I have argued is in congruence with the
Christian experience, which, having been experienced
mostly from a male perspective, has tended to assume
a centered selfhood that needs transformation rather
than realize the need to call a self into being.
Thus, I have suggested that the Christian experience
of liberation to full humanity, which is the call to
the empowerment to be fully human, should be
expressed more adequately than as a call to service
and altruism.

Rosemary Radford Ruether in Sexism and God
Talk: Toward a Feminist Theology argues, on the
other hand, that service and altruism--or what she
calls servanthood--was a liberating notion for the
early Christian community and can be one today.
Ruether does note that there has been a danger in the
call to servanthood, for as Christianity became in
history the religion of the Roman Empire and "human
hierarchies of powers [were seen] as expressions of
Christ's reign," the language of servanthood was used
"to reinforce, in Christ's name, the servitude of
subjugated people."[43] Yet Ruether declares that:

In its use by Jesus appropriated from the
prophetic tradition, it means that God
alone is father and king and we, therefore,
owe no allegiance to human fathers and
kings. As servants of God alone, we are
freed from servitude to human hierarchies
of power.[44]

Thus, she argues, the language of servanthood
suggests the opposite of servanthood--namely that
"domination and subjugation will be overcome."[45]
Servanthood means that relationships between people
are ones not of domination but of mutuality.
Moreover, Ruether argues that in Christianity this
non-hierarchical notion of reality extends as well to
God. In the Kingdom of God, she notes, "people will
no longer model social or religious relationships, or
even relationships to God, after the sort of power
that reduces others to servility."[46] Rather,
"Jesus' image of God and Christ as Servant transforms
all relations including relations to God."[47] Thus,

121

Ruether argues that servanthood of a God who is a servant means the end to structures of domination and the establishment of systems of mutuality.

The language of servanthood, as Ruether calls it, means not only that there shall be no hierarchies, no domination, and no servility. It also means that a new concept of power begins to inform relationality. Power is no longer power over, but empowerment. People in the Kingdom of God--in the new community, Ruether says, "will discover a new kind of power, a power exercised through service, which empowers the disinherited and brings all to a new relationship of mutual enhancement."[48] One's service of another brings that other empowerment--an empowerment that is meant to correct the injustices that domination and oppression create. This notion of power is new, for it understands that empowerment means engendering power in others and not holding it over others. This power is engendered by serving another, by recognizing that other's need to be empowered, by refusing to assume a position of dominance over that person but instead enhancing their own dignity by serving them, by treating that person's needs as important, by listening to that person's words of self-expression. Moreover, because all are served, this empowerment is mutual.

Within the community of redeemed, in the Kingdom of God, Ruether notes, all will be/are servants. And just as within the community the language of servanthood means empowerment and not servility, so the relationship to a society that exists by domination of the subjugated is not to be one of servility either. Ruether notes:

> Jesus did not mean that he and his followers are to be like servants or slaves as society understands the "good slave," that is, as one who unquestioningly subjects himself or herself to the existing social order of bondage. Jesus uses the term servant for himself and his disciples in a prophetic-messianic sense, presupposing a special relation to God. By becoming a servant of God, one becomes freed of all bondage to human masters. Only then, as a liberated person, can one truly become "servant of all," giving one's life to liberate others rather than to

exercise power and rule over them.[49]

A "servant of all" then is one who uses her/his
freedom, grounded in the act of a God who is shown
through Jesus to be one who relates not through
domination, but through servanthood that
empowers/frees human creatures from structures of
domination, to enhance the freedom of others. This
"servant of all" is not servile--nor is her/his
freedom given up in servanthood. Rather, the
servant's freedom is engaged, invested in the
liberation of another so that freedom and empowerment
might increase. Freed from "earthly" masters who
would enslave, the "servant of all" is free to engage
his/her freedom in the liberation and empowerment of
others. Servanthood means, Ruether argues, not the
suppression of freedom but its contagion.

Moreover, Ruether argues, not only does the
language of servanthood--which includes the notion
that God is a servant--mean empowerment and
liberation rather than servility, it means that
systems of domination should no longer endure. God
as servant, rather than King, denounces those who
have exploited others by such domination. "Jesus as
liberator," Ruether says,

> . . . calls for a renunciation, a
> dissolution, of the web of status
> relationships by which societies have
> defined privilege and deprivation. He
> protests against the identification of this
> system with the favor or disfavor of God.
> His ability to speak as liberator does not
> reside in his maleness but in the fact that
> he has renounced this system of domination
> and seeks to embody in his person the new
> humanity of service and mutual
> empowerment.[50]

Speaking theologically, Ruether suggests:

> Jesus as the Christ, the representative of
> liberated humanity and the liberating Word
> of God, manifests the kenosis of patriarchy,
> the announcement of the new humanity
> through a lifestyle that discards
> hierarchical caste privilege and speaks on
> behalf of the lowly.[51]

123

And this same Jesus is one who, Ruether says, "speaks to and is responded to by low-caste women because they represent the bottom of this status network. . . ."[52]

This kenosis (or emptying) of patriarchy that Jesus manifests is not, however, Ruether notes, a kenosis of self or of the empowerment of selfhood. Rather servanthood, or ministry, is the emptying not of self but of power over others. Servanthood, (Diaconia)

> . . . is kenotic or self-emptying of power as domination. Ministry transforms leadership from power over others to empowerment of others. The abdication of power as domination has nothing to do with servility. The call to ministry is not a call to become the passive supporter of the public order or the toady of the powerful in the Church or society. Rather, ministry means exercising power in a new way, as a means of liberation of one another. Service to others does not deplete the person who ministers, but rather causes her (or him) to become more liberated. Ministry overcomes competitive one-up, one-down relationships and generates relations of mutual empowerment.[53]

Far from engendering servility, servanthood should "draw out the unique gifts of each person in the community and give each person the confidence and skills to develop these gifts for the sake of the others."[54] Servanthood, thus, is not the self-emptying of the self that a life lived totally "in and for others" would suggest. Rather it is the self-emptying of "power as domination"--the emptying of a selfhood that would live "over-against"--and it is the affirmation of self as one begins "exercising power in a new way." One does not become emptied of self but learns to be a self in a new way. One does not abdicate the power of selfhood, but learns to use that power in a new way. This means that the self that is "self-emptying of power as domination" is becoming a new self and that relations between persons are changing as well. The self emptied of power as domination still is empowered, not empowered "as opposed to" but empowered through a new confidence to develop her/his own talents and

124

abilities. And because the nature of this new self that knows power as empowerment is not "closed off" or "over against" but rather open and relational, the empowering experience enhances not only the new self, but those in the community as well. Empowerment is described by servanthood. It is never for the self alone but is also "for the sake of others."

Can this notion of servanthood as explained by Ruether be empowering for women? Women we have seen, experience the need for liberation from the context of a patriarchy that would "name" us and teach us servility and submission. The notion of servanthood as developed by Ruether would speak to women's liberation in several ways. First, it speaks of a liberation from "earthly masters" and earthly systems. No longer must women submit to a system as God-ordained. Second, it speaks of servanthood to the oppressed and servile--a servanthood that identifies the cause of the oppressed as the cause of God. Jesus came and dwelt among the oppressed. Emptied of patriarchal prerogatives, he was incarnate, through servanthood, as one of them. Servanthood means that the cause of liberation is to be served. Third, servanthood means an end to domination and the advent of a new form of power--not power over, but power to empower. It would seem then that the Christian understanding of God as servant, Jesus as servant, would indeed seek to empower those who have been oppressed and in servitude through the announcement both that God's judgment is upon systems of domination and that God's empowerment is known through God's servanthood--through the empowering of the dominated.

Moreover, servanthood, as Ruether describes it, means not servility but rather relationships without domination. It points against power as domination and toward power as mutual empowerment. When power is dominating power, it is understood as power "from above"--power which the dominant use to keep the oppressed oppressed. In the context of a divinely ordained scheme, the power of the powerful emanates from God. Whatever power there is is "mediated" from above. But a community characterized by servanthood--by service and altruism--has no domination--and thus no leader through whom power is mediated. In the Christian community even the one they knew as leader was servant of all. Thus, in a community characterized by servanthood power does not

125

come from above but wells up in the midst of the
community.

Thus, Ruether has effectively argued that the
Christian experience of a servant God can be
empowering to the powerless by affirming God's
solidarity with their cause, God's presence among
them, and God's judgment of systems of oppression.
She has shown how the kenosis of patriarchal
prerogatives can mean a new form of relationality
that means not power over but empowerment--where each
serves the needs of the others in mutuality. But has
she shown how servanthood can be liberating to
women? Has she shown how the call to servanthood can
call women to speak in our own voices?

On the one hand she has claimed to do just
that. Women are called to be servants of God and
thus are to be liberated from human masters.
Moreover, we are to be servants of a God who serves
the cause of the oppressed. Thus she has shown how
the concept of a God who chooses to empower, rather
than have power over, can be empowering to oppressed
people. As servants of the oppressed, women would be
able to serve our own cause.

However, has she shown how servanthood--putting
the needs of others and the community first--can
empower women? Servanthood, she has argued means a
kenosis--an emptying. Although she argues that this
kenosis is not of self but of power over, I would
suggest that the very use of the word kenosis
suggests that Ruether assumes a self that is not to
be emptied. The word kenosis and the accompanying
"emptied not of self" suggests that the self is there
but not to be emptied. It does not suggest that a
self is called into being. Ruether's affirmation is
that those who have a self that is established
through power over others are to be emptied of that
type of power and be transformed into a new type of
self that seeks to spark a contagious empowerment in
others. And it is the affirmation that those who
have had a weak sense of self are not called through
servanthood to an emptying of that self. Rather,
through membership in a community of mutual
servanthood, those with weak selves are offered
empowerment of their selves. Thus, she has suggested
that mutual service can be empowering.

But I would argue that although women's sense of

126

self has been termed weak, we have seen that women's experience of selfhood would be better termed negated, lost. Women's selfhood cannot be assumed. To be selves in a community of mutuality, women first need to be called to hear our own voices--to find ourselves. Mutual caring in a community where all are served without the call to hear our own voices, I would argue, would not empower women. Rather, women must first be called to give voice to our own needs and explore our own talents before we are able to participate equally in a relationship of mutuality. Put in a situation where all are to be served, we have seen, women without a center from which to know our own needs tend to serve others without claiming service for ourselves. Once women find our voices, then relationships of mutuality rather than ones of dominance/submission, would describe a community in which we could be continually empowered.[55]

Ruether herself seems to realize this when she says that persons must first be "freed of all earthly masters" before they can serve others. Only then, as a liberated person, can one truly become a "servant of all." It is not, then, servanthood that liberates, but the call of God to liberation. Mutual servanthood "presupposes a special relation to God." It has been this special call of God that has liberated women. This has been the call for women, Ruether says, "to preach, to teach, to form a new community where women's gifts were fully actualized. . . ."[56]

Furthermore, I would question whether servanthood adequately describes the community of empowerment Ruether envisions. Is a community where no one dominates and none are servile accurately characterized as a community of servants? Is servanthood an adequate way of describing the experience of mutual empowerment? I would suggest not. The relationship of mutual empowerment--of a care for others that sparks their own contagious freedom--is better described in another way.[57] Moreover, I would question whether the service and altruism--by which the liberated community is called to be characterized--can truly empower the oppressed to their full human freedom. That is, I question whether one can "serve" others to their liberation. Rather, I would suggest that "service" of the oppressed suggests the development of patterns of dependency that are not liberating at all.[58]

127

Dorothee Soelle has suggested that "every attempt to humanize suffering must . . . activate forces that enable a person to overcome the feeling that he is without power."[59] To liberate another, one must enable that other to experience his/her own power. Servanthood, Jürgen Moltmann argues, cannot bring about such an empowerment. Rather, it subverts such an empowerment. Servanthood, he suggests, seems to be "actually false and a concealed form of domination."[60]

> As long as a church regards itself as a "servant church," as a "church for the nation," or a "church for the world," or a "church for others," it will always regard the subjectivity and adulthood of those it "cares for" as a threat to itself.[61]

Servanthood does not liberate people to adulthood, to their own power, but creates in them a need to be served, a dependency. Christians, on the other hand "are in the first place simply 'with others.' Only as those who delight in life with others do they then, when need arises, also sacrifice themselves 'for others.'"[62] Christians are primarily to be those who are "with" others, accompanying them, delighting in their new-found subjectivity, their self-centering, their new voices. Servanthood, living "for others," tends not to accompany but to "do for" and keep the other dependent--in need of more "doing-for." Yet, Moltmann argues:

> Not even Jesus came to fetter human beings to himself by his ministry, to make himself indispensable for them. "Your faith has saved you," he habitually says when people want to thank him for being healed. Your own faith![63]

Even God, Moltmann continues, "exists 'for us' only in our distress, for it is God's will to live 'with us' in eternity. God wants us as 'autonomous human beings'. . . ."[64] Jesus and the God of Jesus, Moltmann argues, are concerned with the empowering of people to "do for" themselves. Thus while Ruether and Schüssler-Fiorenza have suggested that servanthood of the cause of the oppressed can mean liberation from servility, Moltmann argues that it has not pointed to autonomy and self-empowerment but to a dependency upon those who would serve. The true

128

spirit of God, he argues, works to develop not dependency but independency. He concludes, "We should look for the Spirit where human beings become autonomous agents of their own lives and take the initiative for themselves."[65] Moltmann's emphasis on "autonomy" needs to be understood within the context of the entire paper from which these passages are quoted. The entire work is a dialogue entitled "Becoming Human in New Community." The "autonomy" of which he speaks is one within the context of a new community.

If Christianity is about empowerment, as both Schüssler-Fiorenza and Ruether wish to affirm, then we must seriously question whether servanthood--service and altruism--adequately express that empowerment. I have suggested that neither the call to service and altruism, nor the call to be served by a servant community are liberating notions. If Christianity is meant to empower the powerless--to call persons to be "autonomous" agents responsible for themselves, then the intuition of empowerment needs to be expressed in a language other than that of servanthood--of service and altruism.

Mary, in her Magnificat, sings her praises to the God, who, in seeking to bring low the mighty, "has put down the mighty from their thrones" and "exalted those of low degree."[66] And Ruether has said, "The response of faith to this presence of the liberating Gospel calls the oppressed out of servitude and brings them into their inheritance as people of God and heirs of the new age."[67] The lowly and oppressed, she is saying, are not servants but "heirs" as they receive their inheritance, their freedom. In a similar vein, Schüssler-Fiorenza has stated that the basileia vision of Jesus "calls all women without exception to wholeness and selfhood, as well as to solidarity with those women who are impoverished, the maimed, and outcasts of our society and church."[68] Note, she has said wholeness and selfhood "as well as" solidarity with the oppressed. The call to wholeness and selfhood it would seem, then, is not identical with the call to solidarity, to service and altruism, with and for the oppressed.

It would seem then that the liberation experienced through Christianity is not adequately expressed as one of servanthood--of service and altruism--no matter how paradoxically that

servanthood is defined. Rather, Scripture, Moltmann,
Ruether, and Schüssler-Fiorenza point us to a
different description of the experience of
liberation--one of "exaltation," "autonomy,"
"freedom," "inheritance," and "wholeness and
selfhood." The affirmation of selfhood we have
argued in this chapter is central to the Christian
experience. What has been absent in the language of
service and altruism, however, is an actual call to
such a selfhood--the call to speak in one's own
voice. In Chapter V we shall explore the experience
of freedom suggested in these last paragraphs to see
if it can better capture what I have argued in this
chapter are the dual aspects of the Christian vision
of human liberation/fulfillment: a centered self
that lives in vulnerability and concern for
relationships with others.

NOTES

[1]Reinhold Niebuhr, The Nature and Destiny of Man vol. II "Human Destiny" (New York: Charles Scribner's Sons, 1943), p. 110.

[2]Chapter I, pp. 18-20.

[3]Reinhold Niebuhr, The Nature and Destiny of Man vol. I "Human Nature" (New York: Charles Scribner's Sons, 1941), p. 3.

[4]Reinhold Niebuhr, Faith and History: A Comparison of Christian and Modern Views of History (New York: Charles Scribner's Sons, 1949), p. 174.

[5]Niebuhr, "Human Nature," p. viii.

[6]See Niebuhr's discussion of "The Christian View of Man" in "Human Nature," pp. 12-18. Humanity realizes its true transcendence when it is known from "beyond" itself from the perspective of God.

[7]Niebuhr, "Human Nature," p. 16.

[8]Ibid., p. 178.

[9]Niebuhr, "Human Nature," p. 110.

[10]Ibid., pp. 108-9.

[11]Ibid., pp. 113-114. "Yet when the sinful self is broken and the real self is fulfilled from beyond itself, the consequence is a new life rather than destruction. In the Christian doctrine the self is therefore both more impotent and more valuable, both more dependent and more indestructible than in the alternate doctrines."

[12]As Roy Fairchild suggests in his interpretation of the same passage of Scripture from which Niebuhr borrows the motif of crucifixion and shattering (Gal 2:20-21): "The Apostle Paul testifies: 'I have been crucified with Christ; now I live, no longer I' (in the old sense), 'but Christ lives in me.' This would appear to put the ego pretty well out of the picture, but he follows up with these words, which reinstate the ego: 'I live in faith; faith in the Son of God who loves me and gave himself for me.' He then proceeds into a tirade

which begins, 'Are you people in Galatia mad?' and
continues to castigate them for their behavior and
attitudes. Clearly he has an ego strong enough to
make judgments!" Roy Fairchild, "Spiritual Guidance
in Ego-Strengthening Experience," second Schaff
Lecture delivered at Pittsburgh Theological Seminary,
Pittsburgh, PA, Spring 1983, p. 5.

[13]Niebuhr, "Human Nature," p. 288.

[14]Ibid., pp. 288-9.

[15]Ibid., p. 289.

[16]Ibid., p. 57.

[17]Ibid., p. 294.

[18]Ibid., p. 294.

[19]Ibid., pp. 294-5 (emphasis mine).

[20]Jean Baker Miller, Toward a New Psychology
of Women (Boston: Beacon Press, 1976); Carol
Gilligan In a Different Voice: Psychological Theory
and Women's Development (Cambridge, MA: Harvard
University Press, 1982); Anne Wilson Schaef, Women's
Reality: An Emerging Female System in the White Male
Society (Minneapolis, MN: Winston Press, 1981).

[21]For an argument that Jesus came to reveal
the very nature of reality as relationality, see
Isabel Carter Heyward, The Redemption of God: A
Theory of Mutual Relation (Lanham, MD: University
Press of America, 1982).

[22]As Roy Fairchild says: "History is replete
with attempts by Christian spiritual leaders to crush
the ego with its desires, its bodily needs, and its
reflective faculties, all thought at times in
Christian history to be enemies of discipleship. The
words 'deny yourself, take up your cross and follow
me' have frequently been interpreted as a demand for
groveling, self-hatred, and masochism." Fairchild
goes on to illustrate this tendency in the writings
of Athanasius, Thomas a Kempis, and others.
"Spiritual Guidance in Ego-Strengthening
Experiences," pp. 6-7.

[23]Daniel Day Williams, God's Grace and Man's

<u>Hope</u> (New York: Harper & Brothers, 1949), p. 76.

[24]<u>Ibid.</u>, p. 76.

[25]<u>Ibid.</u>, p. 79.

[26]<u>Ibid.</u>, p. 79.

[27]<u>Ibid.</u>, p. 79.

[28]<u>Ibid.</u>, p. 79.

[29]<u>Ibid.</u>, p. 92.

[30]<u>Ibid.</u>, p. 78.

[31]Daniel Day Williams, <u>The Spirit and the</u>
<u>Forms of Love</u> (Washington, DC: University Press of
America, Inc., 1981), p. 209.

[32]<u>Ibid.</u>, p. 116.

[33]<u>Ibid.</u>, p.   .

[34]Paul Tillich, <u>Love, Power, and Justice:</u>
<u>Ontological Analyses and Ethical Applications</u> (New
York: Oxford University Press, 1954).

[35]<u>Ibid.</u>, p. 26.

[36]<u>Ibid.</u>, p. 27.

[37]<u>Ibid.</u>, p. 26.

[38]<u>Ibid.</u>, p. 27.

[39]<u>Ibid.</u>, p. 27.

[40]Tillich uses the term "separate" to describe
the   self-centered   individual.   But   because   for
Tillich, this is a separate <u>center</u> and not a bounded
self as I have suggested is the case for Niebuhr, and
because for Tillich one aspect of everyone's being is
not only individuation but also participation, this
notion of separation does not necessarily entail the
same   experience   as   that   described   earlier   as
"male"--where separate means cut-off.

[41]Tillich, p. 68.

[42] Ibid., p. 69.

[43] Rosemary Radford Ruether, _Sexism and God-Talk: Toward a Feminist Theology_ (Boston: Beacon Press, 1983), p. 28.

[44] Ibid., p. 28.

[45] Ibid., p. 30.

[46] Ibid., p. 30.

[47] Ibid., p. 30.

[48] Ibid., p. 30.

[49] Ibid., p. 121.

[50] Ibid., p. 137.

[51] Ibid., p. 137.

[52] Ibid., p. 137.

[53] Ibid., p. 207.

[54] Ibid., p. 208.

[55] Whereas feminists have argued that love for women must be mutual and not sacrificial (see Andolson's "Agape in Feminist Ethics"), I would concur. However, I would stress that mutuality must mean first of all that a person be able to calculate their own needs and the needs of others--that mutuality not be mutual sacrificial giving. The ability to calculate would reflect in women's experience a state _beyond_ bondage wherein a woman has a center _from_ which to calculate and enter into relationships of mutuality.

[56] Ruether, p. 65.

[57] See Chapter V, p. 157, where I suggest that friendship is a better characterization of the way in which the liberated Christian community can empower the oppressed to claim their full human freedom. Friendship suggests a being "with" the oppressed that does not entail the dependency that an attitude of service can.

[58]See in Chapter III, p. 87, how "service" was used to translate real patterns of manipulation and hidden dependencies in women's experience.

[59]Dorothee Soelle, _Suffering_ (Philadelphia: Fortress Press, 1975), p. 11.

[60]Jürgen Moltmann and Elisabeth Moltmann-Wendel, "Becoming Human in New Community" in _The Community of Women and Men in the Church_ (Philadelphia: Fortress Press, 1983), p. 40.

[61]_Ibid._, p. 40.

[62]_Ibid._, p. 40.

[63]_Ibid._, p. 40.

[64]_Ibid._, p. 40.

[65]_Ibid._, p. 40. Moltmann states: "Only when this 'caring from above' church becomes a community of people will it welcome the autonomous subjectivity of women, of workers, of disabled people, as energy of the spirit." Only when it sees people as people and not as servants or those needing service will people be truly autonomous agents.

[66]Luke 1:47-55.

[67]Ruether, p. 158.

[68]Elisabeth Schüssler Schüssler-Fiorenza, _In Memory of Her: A Feminist Theological Reconstruction of Christian Origins_ (New York: Crossroad, 1983), p. 153.

CHAPTER V

No Longer Slaves But Friends

In the last chapter we explored the meaning of service and altruism as they are understood in Christianity. I argued that whereas service and altruism mean for women the negation of self, within the theologies explored, service and altruism assume and even affirm the self. Service and altruism I then suggested point to a dual focus in what the Christian experience of liberation to full selfhood means: the importance of being a self and the understanding that true selfhood is expressed in a life of vulnerability lived in concern for others as well as the self. But, because service and altruism do not call the self into being--and because from women's experience such a call is necessary if women are to be liberated to our full selfhood by Christianity--I have argued that the liberation experienced in Christianity is characterized inadequately by service and altruism and needs to be expressed in some other way.

We explored as well Rosemary Ruether's argument that membership in a community of servants (which because all are servants and all mutually serve each other, is a community of equals) means not servility but empowerment for all. If all are servants, she has noted, then power is not power-over but power to empower. I noted, however, that it is not servanthood as such but the call of God to liberation that seems to be the liberating factor in the Christian experience of liberation explored by Ruether. The call of God is "prior to" the call to servanthood. And this call, she herself noted, has been known to be a call to teach and preach and create a community in which women can lead. It is a call that exalts the lowly and calls them, as Elisabeth Schüssler Fiorenza has noted,[1] to a freedom and as Jürgen Moltmann noted,[2] to an autonomy that express their liberation to human wholeness. Servanthood seems best then not to characterize the call to liberation but to describe the type of relationship that is to ensue in a community of those liberated by the God of Jesus.

I suggested as well that although service and altruism point to a servanthood that empowers rather than dominates, servanthood does not really empower.

137

Rather, the relationship between the liberated and the lowly, and among the liberated themselves, if it is to be a relationship of empowerment rather than dependency, cannot be expressed by the category of service. As Moltmann has suggested, whereas service and altruism suggest a service for others, the truly liberating and empowering relationship is one that expresses care as a being with others. This notion of being-with means accompanying others and encouraging them on their way. As Dorothee Soelle suggests, the way to overcome powerlessness in another is to "activate forces that enable a person to overcome the feeling that he is without power."[3] Service and altruism, it was argued, do not adequately empower another because the "liberated" one is still dependent and thus without power. Thus, I have suggested, there needs to be another way to describe the relationship between the liberated and the oppressed, and among the liberated themselves--a way that captures the paradoxical nature of servanthood that Ruether has described (i.e., that none are servants, all are equal, and relationships are ones of empowerment)--a way that affirms that the state of liberation is one in which people are "related to" and "with" each other.

The purpose of this chapter is to explore the nature of this "freedom" and "autonomy" that the God of Christianity--it has been suggested--liberates people to claim. What is the nature of this freedom? Can the call to this freedom be one that can empower women to speak in our own voices? And can this theological symbol of freedom be true to the dual notions of what liberated humanity means to Christianity suggested in Chapter IV: that human wholeness is expressed both in being a liberated self and in being a self committed to openness and relationality with others?

In a sermon entitled "The New Covenant of Freedom," Jürgen Moltmann suggests that the God of Christianity is one who "liberates people from tyranny and childish dependence."[4] This God frees people as well "from the imprisonment of sin and the torments of guilt."[5] Freed from the sin of building towers and cutting people off as well as the sin of hiding and dependency, people are called by the God of Christianity, Moltmann argues, to a new state of responsibility for who they are. God leads people "out of their infancy into the full

responsibility of their own history."[6]   God,
Moltmann argues, "does not want slaves or vassals."[7]

> God wants people who have come of age,
> people who make their own decisions and
> take responsibility for what they do.   God
> wants free people, who stand on their own
> feet and are themselves.   God doesn't want
> copies; [God] wants originals.[8]

The God of Christianity, Moltmann suggests, frees
people to "make their own decisions and take
responsibility for what they do." God liberates
people to name themselves, to speak in their own
voices from their own centers of decision.   What is
the nature of this freedom to which the God of
Christianity calls?

In his book To Set At Liberty: Christian Faith
and Human Freedom Delwin Brown explores this
Christian experience of liberation--this call to
freedom.   We shall use Brown's study to begin our
exploration into the nature of the Christian
experience of liberation.   He begins saying those who
experienced "Jesus' gospel of freedom" experienced it
as a gift with many facets, "among them liberation,
obligation, and responsibility."[9]

Freedom, Brown states, as Jesus transmitted it
to others was first of all "in part, a liberation
from various forms of bondage."[10]   Often, he notes,
"no doubt, this liberation was fragmentary.   Often it
came to be refused after initial fascination."[11]
The liberation offered by Jesus, that is, was not
always realized.   Yet he notes, "it was such as to
give rise eventually to a new community which broke
open traditional restrictions of sex, class, piety,
and even family."[12]   The freedom offered by Jesus,
thus, was first of all the liberation from bondage--a
liberation that made possible the creation of a new
community, one without hierarchy and traditional
restrictions, a community of equals.

The gift of freedom, Brown continues, is also
"obligation no less than liberation."[13]   And, "the
direction of freedom's obligation is lived out in
Jesus' clear identification with the poor and the
oppressed."[14]   "That obligation . . . is to serve
the neighbor's need."[15]   Freedom as obligation ties
one's own liberation to the liberation of others.

The notion of obligation, Brown suggests, means a
concern for others that he characterizes as the
obligation to "serve" another's need. Through
freedom one is obliged to be with others and empower
them to freedom. Freedom, that is, does not free one
from connection and concern. Rather, freedom seeks
to transform connections that enforce bondage into
connections that empower greater freedom. The nature
of this "service" is to stimulate not dependency but
the extension of freedom. He notes:

> . . . the source of freedom is tied to the
> extension of freedom; the freedom of one is
> tied to the freedom of all. Therefore, the
> experience of freedom implies the extension
> of freedom everywhere, in whatever form it
> is lacking. That is the obligation of the
> kingdom of freedom. The free community is
> freeing. The one who is being liberated is
> liberating.[16]

The gift of freedom, Brown argues, is finally
the gift of responsibility. But the nature of this
notion of responsibility must be understood "in
relation to Jesus' authority."[17] Jesus, Brown
recalls, was described in Mark 1:22 as one who taught
"as one who had authority, and not as the scribes."
This authority, Brown suggests, is descriptive of
Jesus because he acted "as God alone would act."[18]
That is, "Jesus' claim to authority is a claim to act
from out of himself; it is a claim to freedom."[19]
Thus, Brown is arguing, freedom means acting with
authority--acting not according to another's
authority, but "out of oneself," from one's own
center. And, Brown suggests, "if the New Testament
claims for Jesus a peculiar freedom in the form of
his authority even to forgive sins, it also suggests
that Jesus transmits that authority, that freedom, to
his followers."[20] Brown notes:

> In the controversy over the healing of the
> paralytic of Capernaum, the issue is Jesus'
> authority to forgive sins (Matt 9:6 and
> parallels). Matthew carries the
> extraordinary commentary: "When the crowd
> saw it, they were afraid, and they
> glorified God, who had given such power to
> men" (9:8).[21]

Brown argues: "The power in question is not Jesus'

ability to heal; it is his authority--this is what was given 'to men.'"[22] And, he concludes, that this authority is really for "men" is evident elsewhere as well:

> Matthew 18:18 and John 20:23 both represent Jesus as conferring this power on his disciples. Paul instructs the Corinthians to "deliver . . . to Satan" the man living with his father's wife (1 Cor 5:5), as he himself delivers others "to Satan" (1 Tim 1:20). Finally, insofar as the healings manifest Jesus' authority, the same suggestion may also be found in the statement that the disciples shall do even greater things than Jesus had done (John 14:12).[23]

Although the authority given to his followers by Jesus has been "interpreted along narrowly ecclesiastical lines," Brown argues that "the authority ingredient in Jesus' freedom was experienced as a part of that gift no less than was liberation and obligation. . . ."[24] This means, Brown concludes, that Jesus' followers share in his authority, an "authority of freedom," which "is the responsibility to order the structures of the world, including those of the church in the world."[25] Thus the gift of freedom as responsibility means both the authority to act, and the responsibility to do so.

Drawing from Peter Hodgson, Brown argues that this authority that Jesus shares with his followers--this exousia

> . . . does not mean "authority" in the sense of an authoritarian tradition or law, inherited privilege, physical coercion, or power. Rather it means "freedom" in the sense of "freedom to act" or "original freedom". . . .[26]

This authority of Jesus, Brown says, "is his contextual creativity, i.e., his power to act out of himself, radically remaking the context to which he is nevertheless gratefully indebted."[27] And this transformed context is one that is to engender greater freedom--greater empowerment. Thus, "the gift of Jesus' authority is not his authority over others so much as it is his authority for

141

others."[28] And this authority for others grants to others "their agency, their ability to respond creatively in the world, their responsibility."[29] Jesus' authority is not a new law, it "does not impose restrictions upon freedom."[30] Rather, it creates a new kind of law, a new kind of imperative, for "it articulates what is necessary in order that freedom be preserved and enhanced."[31] Thus, acceptance of the authority Jesus grants and its corresponding responsibility means "to become a steward of freedom in the world, to reorder the world on behalf of freedom."[32] (Note, to be a steward is to be one who from his/her own center of responsibility seeks to engender freedom in the world.) Thus, a call to "obedience" to the new kind of law Jesus gives, to love God and neighbor as self, is the call to share in the freedom of Jesus which is both the authority and the responsibility to create a context where greater freedom can become manifest. This is the responsibility of freedom: both the ability and the obligation to respond in a liberating fashion.

Thus, as Brown has argued, the freedom Jesus offers to others is the freedom from oppression and bondage. It is the freedom from external authorities. It is a freedom to accept one's own authority, to decide from within oneself. It is the freedom to name oneself. But this freedom and authority are contextual because one's authority is expressed within the context both of the given world and of the intention of God to create greater liberty. Thus freedom and authority are understood as the freedom to respond to the world from within one's own center of authority according to one's obligation to work for the creation of greater freedom. Authority and freedom are not authority "over" another--they are rather engaged in creating greater freedom. Thus we can see that the freedom Jesus offers both calls the self into being (the call to have authority) and understands the liberated self to be "obligated" to create an environment where greater freedom may abound. The notion of authority as explored here thus paradoxically means empowerment of others (just as Ruether argues mutual servanthood should do).

Although freedom might suggest the opposite of servanthood (a disengaged, autonomous authority), freedom as Brown describes it (as obligated, engaged

142

freedom), actually includes the same intuition we have discovered through our exploration of the "paradoxical" nature of service and altruism. This engaged freedom is freedom as obligation and as responsibility--freedom that is engaged in the cause of freedom. But freedom suggests something that servanthood--service and altruism--have not. It suggests not only obligation, liberation, and responsibility, but also the ability to respond, the agency and the authority to re-order and transform the world. Jesus empowers his followers not with a new law that demands their submissive obedience, but a new kind of law--a law that frees them and empowers them to transform the context of domination and oppression into a context for freedom. The community of the liberated thus becomes those freed to express their own "contextual creativity," their own authority to re-order and transform the world. The followers of Jesus do this not only through obligation and responsibility for the greater freedom of each other and the oppressed, but as authoritative persons, ordained, chosen by Jesus to be agents of freedom in a world that would deny freedom and institute bondage. This notion of authority takes us beyond servanthood--while not negating its intuitions--for authority is to be responsible and contextual, obligated, and engaged in the cause of liberty. Servanthood, we have seen, means a relationality that empowers rather than overpowers; a personhood that is clearly grounded in the context of the needs and concerns of others; a liberation from bondage to human structures of oppression and servility. Freedom, as described in this chapter, suggests all of these and adds as well the call to become a centered being. The call to freedom offered by Jesus is the call to live from one's own center and with an integrity that can engage the world and re-order it in a better way.

Whereas the language of servanthood has not so much called for the creation of selfhood but has rather assumed a self, through the language of freedom, we have seen that the experience of Jesus by his followers was one of a call to freedom and authority--engaged and creative authority. This authority is the freedom to act from within oneself--the authority to speak and act from one's own center of freedom. The authority that is, I would argue, the authority to be a self.

143

Brown has argued that Jesus shared his authority with his followers and that this authority is what Christianity is about. However, whereas Brown has tended to affirm authority as obligation to describe how one <u>serves</u> others, I would suggest that the notion of authority as he has pursued it takes us beyond servanthood to a state of selfhood that does not serve but rather from its center of authority is able to integrate the "needs of others and the community" within itself and respond in a way that is responsible both to the self (i.e., affirms that <u>it</u> decides and responds within the context of its own needs) and to those for whom it is concerned. Because authority is what freedom is about--the freedom to be an integrated engaged self--then the appropriate response to others is not one of service and dependency but rather one that sparks in others their own center of authority, their own ability to integrate and create their own response.

That Jesus is concerned about calling his followers to their own authority, I would suggest, can be seen in the fifteenth chapter of the Gospel of John. "No longer do I call you servants," the Johannine community remembers Jesus saying, "for the servant does not know what his master is doing: but I have called you friends, for all that I have heard from my Father I have made known to you" (15:15, RSV). This passage suggests that perhaps "friends" may be a better term than "servants" to describe the followers of Jesus--ones who relate to others not by serving them but by sparking them to their own freedom--by sharing with them all that they know. While this passage uses the language of servanthood, the Greek word used for servant is not <u>diakonia</u>--which best translates "servant" as we have been using it--but <u>douloi</u>, which is better translated "slaves." Thus I would suggest that this passage is directly concerned about the issue of the followers of Jesus having authority. This concern is expressed in the tension that is exposed between being "slaves" and being "friends" who "know" what Jesus has shared with them.

First let us pursue a study of the word used for slave in this passage--the word <u>doulos</u>. <u>Doulos</u> or slave connotes a strong passive element. The service of a slave in ancient times was "not a matter of choice for the one who renders it," because the slave "is subject . . . to an alien will, to the will of

144

his owner."[33] In its ancient Greek context, slavery or douleuein means that "human autonomy is set aside and an alien will takes precedence of one's own."[34] Slavery thus stands in opposition, according to the Greek understanding, to freedom and personal identity/autonomy, for "the Greek finds his personal identity in the fact that he is free."[35] And on "Jewish soil" the word group around doulos "expresses with singular force both the extreme of power demanded and exercised on the one side and the extreme of objective subjugation and subjective bondage present and experienced on the other."[36]

As the word was used in the translation of Scripture, it became used for the language of service of God. In the Septuagint douleuein is used for service of God as "total commitment to the Godhead."[37] In the New Testament Jesus "speaks of douloi when He wishes to emphasize the unconditional nature of human responsibility to God (cf. Mt 24:45ff.; Lk 12:37ff.). . . ."[38] But, whereas these examples of the use of doulos are in the parables of Jesus, where servants are the actors in the story, the "formula doulos theou is very little used of Christians in the New Testament. . . ."[39] Rather, "most references to the douleuein of Christians speak of it in relation to Christ. . . ."[40] It is Paul who primarily uses the term. For Paul, Christians were once slaves of sin, but as Christians they are slaves of Christ. The notion of "slave of Christ" is Paul's way of expressing both the liberation Christians experience in Christ and the commitment a Christian feels toward Christ.

Regardless of the way Paul refers to Christians as slaves of Christ, however, Jesus in this passage in John is remembered as calling his followers friends and clearly not slaves, for he tells them "all that I have heard from my Father I have made known to you" (15:15). That is, Jesus has empowered his disciples with his knowledge of God--they then are not to be slaves, passive and subject to an alien will, but friends. What Jesus means by friend here is one who knows. And when "friends" is put in tension with "slaves," the emphasis is on those who not only know but who then act from their own center of will--not according to an alien one, not one from without. Jesus' followers were friends who knew the intentions of the God of Jesus and who, in the context of the world, were to respond from their own

145

centers, informed by the knowledge shared by Jesus. This saying of Jesus then points to the very authority Brown has suggested Jesus gave his followers: the authority to act out of themselves, to act from their own center, and not according to an alien one.

This authority to which Jesus calls his followers, this state of knowing and acting from their own center, is an authority deeply grounded in their relationship/friendship with Jesus. It is a contextual authority--a contextual freedom. Jesus says in John 15:5: "I am the vine, you are the branches. He who abides in me, and I in him, he it is that bears much fruit, for apart from me you can do nothing." This knowledge, this friendship, this authority, is rooted to the vine, to the body of Christ, to the community of followers of Jesus. It is not an authority over-against--it is not an authority unto itself--it is a responsive authority, the authority to respond from one's own center within the context of the vine, the community, the mission and knowledge of Jesus. This responsive authority thus is a gift, for it comes out of a relationship/friendship with Jesus and always exists within the context of that relationship.

But there appears to be a tension between the Johannine affirmation that followers of Jesus are to be friends and not slaves and the Pauline assertion that Jesus' followers are to be slaves of Christ. Paul's language seems to oppose the claim that the freedom Jesus offers his followers gives them authority to speak from their own centers rather than living according to an alien will. As one interpreter understands Paul, to be a slave of Christ means that one is redeemed to a state "which is obedience rather than autonomy."[41] In the work of redemption, Christ "makes the redeemed His own possession, giving them directions and goals by which to shape their lives."[42] God is understood to demand "unconditional commitment" so that by God's "work and word [God] exercises sovereign rule over the relationship of man to God and God to man, and therefore over man's whole conduct within the ordinary nexus of life."[43]

However, although Paul uses the language of slavery to Christ, in understanding what slavery to Christ means for Paul we must consider it within the context of its Pauline opposite: slavery to sin. In Paul's letters, persons are either slaves of sin or slaves of Christ. Whereas slavery to sin is understood through metaphors of bondage and slavery, slavery to Christ means not slavery but freedom. Galatians 5:1 reads: "For freedom Christ has set us free; stand fast therefore, and do not submit again to a yoke of slavery." The freedom offered in Christ is of course totally grounded in one's relationship to Christ; it is in Christ that people are free. But in Christ persons are free. In Christ persons are free from bondage to sin and death. Whereas bondage to sin has meant bondage to an alien will, in freedom from sin, Rudolf Bultmann notes, "the believer gains life and thereby his own self."[44] No longer subject to an alien will, the one in Christ is subject of his/her own will.

This interpretation of Paul's view of the believer's relationship to Christ as one of freedom is buttressed by the Pauline assertion that in Christ persons are freed as well from the Law. Persons in Christ are freed from subjection to the Law to a state of "authorization." As Bultmann interprets Paul's understanding of freedom from the Law, "out of Christian 'freedom' flows 'authorization' (exousia), which is expressed in 'all things are lawful for me' (which could just as well be translated: 'for me all things are authorized')."[45] In Chapter II we noted that Elisabeth Schüssler Fiorenza states that Christians are called to freedom, for "where the Spirit of the Lord is there is freedom" (Gal 5:13). And she said this freedom is one which "sums up the Christian's situation before God as well as in this world."[46] Thus we can conclude that the notion of slavery to Christ found in the Pauline corpus means not bondage to an alien will but freedom and a certain authority--exousia. Moreover, followers of Christ are characterized in the Pauline corpus not only as slaves of Christ but as "heirs"--those who receive not the "spirit of slavery" but "the spirit of sonship." Paul says:

> For all who are led by the Spirit of God are sons of God. For you did not receive the spirit of slavery to fall back into fear, but you have received the spirit of sonship. When we cry, "Abba! Father!" it is the Spirit himself bearing witness with our spirit that we are children of God, and

147

if children, then heirs, heirs of God and
fellow heirs with Christ, provided we
suffer with him in order that we may also
be glorified with him.[47]

Thus, although Paul refers to Jesus' followers as
"slaves" and not as "friends" as the Johannine
writing suggests, the tension between the two
expressions does not involve a contradiction in the
meaning. In fact, Paul himself seems to affirm a
sense of authority grounded in Christ, an authority
similar to the one I have argued is suggested in John
15. This authority is in principle a refusal of
subjection to patriarchal rules and authorities,
despite Paul's own failure to develop its
implications in this direction.

The pericope within which John 15:15 is found
begins with verses 12-14:

This is my commandment, that you love
one another as I have loved you. Greater
love has no man than this, that a man lay
down his life for his friends. You are my
friends if you do as I command you.

Do these verses within the Johannine pericope
contradict the assertion that Jesus' followers were
to be centered selves who speak with their own
voices, from their own centers of authority? Do the
statements calling Jesus' followers to "lay down
their lives" and to be "obedient" to "commands" he
has shared undercut the notion of friendship where a
friend is understood as one who has an inner
authority to know and act from within him/herself?
One commentator has argued that it does. Although in
15:15 "Jesus makes it crystal clear that He is not
bringing His own to a state of douleia, but to
perfect fellowship with Himself," he argues, verse 14
also makes it clear that "fellowship with Him implies
that His own should do what he commands them (15:14),
and that it is broken if obedience is withheld."[48]
He concludes: this insight in verse 15 "is the
insight of Paul. He and John are firmly agreed in
their basic assessment of what is made of disciples
by the act of Jesus."[49]

But let us take the verses separately, focusing
on verse 13: "Greater love has no man than this,
that a man lay down his life for his friends." Verse

148

13 must be seen in the context of verse 15 where Jesus says that to be a friend is to know "all" about this friend. To Jesus this means that his friends shared in all his knowledge about God. Friendship means an intimate revealing between friends. As another commentator, Arthur John Gossip, suggests:

> Friendship . . . consists in a frank unhesitating opening of one's heart and whole mind to the other, without shyness of secretiveness. . . . For to practice friendship worth the name, we must allow the other to see right in and know us as we really are, unstintedly sharing with him what we ourselves have learned.[50]

Friends thus know each other and they are known by each other. They are aware of--and perhaps even share--each other's feelings. In this context of friendship Jesus says in verse 13 that "greater love has no man than this, that a man lay down his life for his friend." Friendship thus means, Gossip suggests, a "willingness to spend oneself for the other"; it means being "so ready to help that he will give and give, his very life if need be, to aid and save his friend."[51]

Does the "willingness to spend oneself" for another "if need be" contradict Jesus' statement that his followers are not to be slaves, not to be obedient to an alien will, but friends, acting from their own centers? Not at all, for I would suggest that a life given "if need be" for the life of a friend might be the highest statement of friendship. The friendship offered by Jesus means the call to an authority, but this authority is a contextual authority. One who is a friend of Jesus, who has the authority called into being by Jesus, engages his/her freedom in the act of transforming and re-ordering the world for greater freedom. This is an authority that, in remaining rooted to the vine, shares the pain of bondage of others and is obligated to make possible more freedom and more empowerment in the world. "If need be," a friend "willingly" may die for another--not as a statement of slavery; not as blind obedience to an alien will; but as an act from one's own center, according to one's own authority.

But what about verse 14, where Jesus says that his friends are those who "do what I command you"?

Does the fact that Jesus "commands" his friends contradict the understanding that friends are ones who know and act from an authority within themselves? Does the "commandment" of Jesus in verse 12 (and also in verse 17) that "you love one another as I have loved you," mean that friendship with Jesus points to a blind obedience? Jesus says, just as he has been their friend, sharing all he knew with them, freeing them from their own slavery, so they must be friends to others, engaging their freedom for them, sharing all they know, re-ordering the world in an act of love that creates in the world new possibilities for freedom. The command of Jesus, thus understood, appears more like a description of the obligation entailed in the freedom offered by Jesus to his followers. The command to love as they have been loved describes what their freedom is to mean--the contagion that results through the call to freedom and empowerment as one, by the very nature of that freedom, works to beget freedom and empowerment in another. As Gossip says: Jesus asks "that we should reproduce this spirit that we find in him, not only toward himself, but to all among whom we live."[52] The fact that Jesus "commanded" his disciples must be understood in parallel with the notion that Jesus also empowers his disciples with authority to act from within themselves. To be Jesus' friend (which one is if he/she does what Jesus commands) is to be called to an "intimate and wholehearted relationship" with him.[53] This relationship is one in which all parties are open to each other and share with each other--trusting each other--taking a risk with each other. The knowledge Jesus shared, the commands he gave to his friends, are not mere laws to which one gives "mere obedience."[54] Such "mere obedience" would be "a slave's part" and Jesus clearly is telling his followers that they are not to be slaves.[55] Rather, as Gossip suggests, "we are summoned to something warmer and more spontaneous. . . ."[56] As friends Jesus' followers are to move beyond "mere obedience" to a spontaneity grounded in the friendship of Jesus.

In her book <u>Beyond Mere Obedience</u> Dorothee Soelle suggests as does Gossip that Christianity is a religion that moves people beyond "mere obedience" to a spontaneity that comes from their own center of being. Christianity is not about slavery, not about "mere obedience" at all. A religion based on "mere obedience" Soelle calls an authoritarian religion. Such a religion that focuses on obedience, she argues, "presupposes duality: one who speaks and one who listens; one who knows and one who is ignorant; a ruler and ruled ones."[57] But Jesus, as we have seen, overcomes such duality. He came not as ruler, but emptied of prerogatives, as servant and friend. He pitched his tent and dwelled among his friends. He was enfleshed in a body like theirs and felt their pain as well as his own. He came not only to speak, but to listen. He shared his knowledge with his friends so that they, too, might act with an inner authority, not one imposed from without as in the case of ignorant slaves. Understanding God through Jesus in a Christocentric way, Soelle says, leads her to know that Christianity, despite its various symbols that have tended to reinforce such authoritarianism (i.e., father-child; king-slaves) has within it a non-authoritarian vision. Soelle finds this vision expressed in the language of the mystics:

> "Source of all that is good," "life-giving wind," "water of life," "light" are all symbols of God which do not imply power of authority and do not smack of any chauvinism. There is no room for "supreme power," domination, or the denial of one's own validity in the mystical tradition.[58]

Such a vision of God, she argues, replaces the lord-servant relation between God and humanity and between humans as well, with one of "agreement and consent, of being as one with what is alive.[59] What one feels toward God, then, is not obedience, but beyond obedience to a state of "solidarity." Just as friends are those who share an intimate knowledge of each other, so, in solidarity with God, God's love permeates one's being, becoming the source and ground for a new spontaneity. A new action, totally responsive to the grace of God that is its ground, yet grounded as well in the authority of one's own being, is born. One's own authoritative center is not made submissive by such an indwelling God, for, Soelle suggests, God is experienced not as an authoritarian ruler, but rather as one who becomes vulnerable and takes the risk of loving persons into their fullness of possibility--who grounds and yet risks human freedom, human spontaneity. Yet, this

151

freedom and spontaneity are neither "absolute" nor
autonomous--for in relying on the grace of God, on
Jesus as the vine, for its nurture, it is a
freedom/spontaneity that springs out of its context
while remaining deeply committed to "what is alive."
The life of spontaneous freedom is one that knows a
new life through the grace of God and responds by
transforming and re-ordering the world in order that
greater life--greater freedom--might be possible.

This "liberated spontaneity" (which Soelle says
is what is meant by "obedience in the proclamation of
Jesus"[60]), frees one from an irresponsible
conformity that "mere obedience" might suggest. Such
conformity removes the actor from the realm of
responsibility, for one's response is not truly one's
own, coming from within. Liberated spontaneity is
precisely responsible. It understands that "the Son
of Man has no place to lay his head" because in
history a commitment to what is alive is a commitment
to grow--and thus to outgrow old rooms, old answers,
old places to safely lay one's head. Thus "obedience
in the proclamation of Jesus" moves beyond mere
obedience, for it is engaged in growth and in the
ongoingness of history. Jesus met people where they
were, confronted them with this knowledge, and called
them to respond. Similarly, the followers of Jesus
are to create their own response given the context of
the world and the knowledge Jesus has shared with
them. "It is not God in a general, timeless sense
who demands obedience, but the situation which
demands a response, and only therein does God require
a person's response."[61] Soelle continues, "Since
the will of God cannot be determined in advance, nor
the situation anticipated, the response the person
makes can only be a decision in the now."[62] This
means that "the person herself must decide what is to
be done; she is not the fulfiller of assigned
commands."[63] And, she concludes, "nothing is here
taken from the autonomy of the subject."[64]

For Jesus, Soelle insists, "'God' meant
liberation, the unchaining of all powers which lie
imprisoned in each of us. . . ."[65] Liberated to a
new spontaneity grounded in the grace of God, each
person knows the release of powers, "powers with
which we too can perform miracles which are no less
significant than those we are told Jesus himself
performed."[66] This spontaneity, this power to
transform the world, is grounded both in the grace of

152

God and in the authoritative center of a person's
being--the center from which she decides rather than
re-acts; from which she speaks with her own voice,
and from which she engages her freedom in a creative
spontaneity committed to "what is alive"--to the
engendering of new life, new power, new spontaneous
freedom in others. Jesus thus acts to liberate
persons from the chains within and without that keep
them from realizing their own power, their own
center, their own voice.

Soelle says, "I consider Jesus of Nazareth the
person most conscious of his own identity."[67]
Likewise, those liberated by Jesus to a spontaneity
of their own discover their own identity--their own
selfhood. Beyond mere obedience, then, is the call
to be a self--a spontaneous fulfilled person. But,
the selfhood engendered thus by the liberating
presence of Jesus is grounded in spontaneity. It is
not static or rigid. It is open both to others and
to its own creativity. Such a self--open to creative
imagination, "conceives of some new possibility and
repeatedly burst the boundaries which limit people,
setting free those who have submitted themselves to
these boundaries which thereby have been endlessly
maintained."[68] Such a self does not "lose itself"
by engaging itself in such a liberating action.
Rather, the act to generate spontaneity, freedom, in
another is an act of spontaneity, an expression of
selfhood engendered from the very center of
spontaneity. The fulfillment of selfhood, Soelle
says,

> . . . liberates the self from its
> established boundaries. Fulfillment
> destroys the prisons which limit the self
> and channel its energies. Once freed, they
> thrust themselves into the adventure of new
> life--in the phantasy which produces
> freedom and devises opportunities for
> others to experience true selfhood.[69]

Thus I have argued that the "command" of Jesus
for his followers to love one another must be seen in
the context of his insistence that they be friends
and not slaves. The command of Jesus is not a
command demanding "mere obedience," which Soelle says
would characterize an authoritarian religion, one
based on the duality between one who knows and one
who is ignorant, which imposes an alien will upon the

ignorant. By sharing what he knew with his
followers, Jesus overcame the duality, closed the gap
between the one who knows and the one who is
ignorant, and thus did not enforce his will as an
alien will upon others. Rather, the "command" of
Jesus should be understood as a call to live "beyond
mere obedience" in a freedom and spontaneity grounded
in the free and spontaneous act of God in Jesus that
releases one to generate freedom and spontaneity in
others. The followers of Jesus, thus, are not to be
merely obedient but persons liberated to generate
from their own center of integrity the freedom of
others.

Jesus, then I would suggest, is one who makes
people his friends, engendering a new authority, a
free spontaneity in them, calling them into
selfhood. This is the "as well as" that we have
intuited in Chapter IV is assumed in the language of
service and altruism. Jesus liberates people from
the chains that would bind their own energies, their
own power. He removes the gag that has cut off their
voices. He unbinds their feet that they may walk,
and run and rejoice in a new spontaneity. He does
not subject them to an alien will, but calls them
friends and calls them to a new authority, a new
freedom--a freedom grounded in an intimate relation
to him.

The authority grounded in the friendship of
Jesus and the spontaneous selfhood that it expresses
are in no way cut off, self-contained, absolutely
autonomous. This self is not the problematic self
Niebuhr identifies through the sin of pride. This is
a freedom that is grounded in the freedom of others
and in turn grounds the freedom of still others.
Spontaneity begets spontaneity; freedom, freedom.
Freedom and spontaneity are never a "given" but are
rather a "gift"--a gift both of the empowering grace
of God and of the spontaneous freedom of others. Yet
this groundedness in no way detracts from the
authority, the centeredness, of the person who
responds to liberation by naming herself and speaking
in her own voice to the unique situation that is her
own. Awakened to her own spontaneity, she becomes a
spark to enflame others with a spontaneity of their
own.

We have seen in Chapters II and IV, in the work
of Rosemary Ruether and Elisabeth Schüssler Fiorenza,

that the God of Christianity is one who liberates people from their oppression by patriarchy. The God who beckons and calls, we have seen in the work of Mary Daly, is one who is involved in women's liberation. The purpose of this book has been to explore the question of whether Christianity can empower women to speak in our own voices. To do so, we have asked whether the call to be a follower of Jesus, in the community of Jesus, is one that can empower women today. In Chapter II we argued through Ruether and Schüssler-Fiorenza that Christianity can in fact offer women a usable tradition and a history of liberation from patriarchal systems. In Chapter III we argued, however, that the theological symbols of service and altruism--meaning putting the needs of others and the community first--are not liberating to women, are not usable for our liberation but, in fact, work against that liberation. In Chapter IV, having viewed service and altruism from the perspective of Christian theologies--theologies written mostly from the assumption of male experience--we have discovered that service and altruism have meant both the affirmation/assumption of the self and the insistence that <u>that</u> self be a vulnerable, relational one. Thus, I have suggested that there are dual aspects to the meaning of service and altruism--and thus to the community in which the God of Christianity calls people to discover their liberation--and that Christianity may very well be about the empowerment of women after all. However, because service and altruism cannot so empower women, I have argued that we have needed to move beyond them to a different theological symbol--a "prior" symbol--of what the Christian community and experience of liberation is all about--yet a symbol that is inclusive of the intent of service and altruism.

I have shown in this chapter that this theological symbol "beyond" service and altruism is one that is suggested by the language of freedom and authority that has appeared in the work of Ruether and Schüssler-Fiorenza as an experience "prior-to" or "as well as" the experience of service and altruism. This language of freedom and authority appears in the work of Schüssler-Fiorenza and Ruether as accompanying that of service and altruism in the expression of what Christian liberation is all about.

In exploring the theological symbols of freedom

155

and the authority Jesus offered in his call to friendship, we have discovered that the freedom and selfhood engendered by Jesus are deeply contextual and relational. The freedom Jesus makes possible is characterized by obligation as well as liberation, responsibility as well as authority. Moreover, the authority to which friends of Jesus are called is not a dis-engaged autonomous authority, but a contextual authority, intimately connected to its source in the friendship of Jesus and intimately concerned by its very nature to spontaneously spark freedom and authority in another. This freedom and selfhood by their very nature reflect the same concern for the liberation of others that has been suggested by service and altruism. That is, freedom and authority as we have described them in this chapter are inclusive of the intentions of service and altruism. The self created and affirmed in this freedom and authority is one that is to be by nature vulnerable, permeable, and spontaneously concerned for others. I would conclude, thus, that the theological symbols of freedom and authority grounded in the friendship of Jesus as a way of describing the community of friends who follow Jesus presume the notions of service and altruism. Moreover, I would suggest that freedom, authority, and friendship are a more adequate way to express the dual notions I have argued are central to the Christian experience of liberation: the call to selfhood and the affirmation that that selfhood is vulnerable, deeply committed to relationality, and aware of the needs of others.

Service and altruism have been problematic for two reasons. The first is that they do not call people to selfhood, but rather assume that selfhood. This has been particularly problematic, as I have argued, in the case of women. Service and altruism do not call women to hear our own voices, find our centers, and speak in our own voices. Rather, they encourage women to continue to hear voices other than our own. Thus, secondly, they have served to encourage women's bondage to alien wills and have effectively blocked women's liberation.

In pursuing the theological symbols of freedom and authority grounded in the friendship of Jesus in this chapter we have discovered that the freedom Christ calls his followers to is the freedom from subjection to an alien will and the freedom to speak and act from their own centers, with their own

156

authority and voices. This, I would argue, is in
fact an understanding that can empower women to speak
in our own voices. Women too easily live lives of
vulnerability. Attentive to voices of others, we
silence our own and become subjected to the needs of
others. This, I have suggested, amounts to
subjection to an alien will (or wills, which is more
likely the case). This "invasion" is compounded by a
patriarchal system which discourages women from
hearing our own voices and speaking with our own
authority, and consigns women to live subject both to
the wills of the voices we are attentive to and to
the authority of patriarchy that decides and judges
for us what our activity/name could and should be.
Moreover, as Daly has noted, this alien will has
invaded women's own inner space. The call of Jesus
to a freedom that is friendship, we have seen, is not
the call to be subject to alien wills but the call to
speak from one's own center according to one's own
authority. This call, I would suggest, would be one
that would mean liberation and selfhood for women.
For this reason, I would argue that the call to
freedom and authority grounded in the friendship of
Jesus is a better way to characterize the call to
Jesus' followers and the community that grows out of
the friendship of Jesus.

Moreover, I would argue that freedom and
authority grounded in friendship with Jesus are a
better way to characterize the community of followers
of Jesus than service and altruism. Whereas we have
seen that service and altruism lead not to freedom
but to dependency on the part of the one served, the
freedom grounded in friendship offered by Jesus leads
not to dependency but a spontaneous freedom and
authority. Those who would follow the "command" of
Jesus to love their friends into freedom are to do so
in the manner of Jesus, not as servants, but as
friends. Thus the community of the followers of
Jesus, I would suggest, would be more accurately and
effectively characterized as a community of friends
who seek not to serve but to befriend the world. As
Jürgen Moltmann suggests, such a community engenders
freedom in others by being "with" them, sharing with
them their own stories of liberation just as Jesus
shared with his followers all he knew, sharing their
own spontaneous freedom, and accompanying them as
they make the knowledge shared by Jesus their own,
and begin to respond from their own centers of
spontaneity.

And because the friends of Jesus are also friends of God, I would suggest that the same empowering experience of an immediate God that Ruether has argued is liberating in the notion of servanthood is available to those who would be friends. Jürgen Moltmann notes, "In the fellowship of Jesus the disciples become friends of God."[70] This means that they "no longer experience God as Lord, nor only as Father; rather they experience [God] in [God's] innermost nature as Friend."[71] The friendship of God means that "the relationship of men and women to God is no longer the dependent, obedient relation of servants to their masters. Nor is it anymore the relation of children to a heavenly Father."[72] Friendship with God means liberation from dependency to a state of reciprocity with God. God, also, then is known as vulnerable and caring and personally involved with each one. As William Barclay has said:

> Jesus called us to be His friends and the friends of God. That is a tremendous offer. It means that no longer do we need to gaze longingly at God from afar off; we are not like slaves who have no right whatever to enter into the presence of the master. . . . Jesus did the amazing thing--He gave us this intimacy with God, so that God is no longer a distant stranger, but our intimate friend.[73]

Thus I would suggest that the friendship of God means the same direct empowering relationship to God that Rosemary Ruether suggests without the dependency that servanthood might entail.[74]

The concern of this chapter has been to explore the freedom that is offered by Jesus. Through this exploration we were to consider two questions: whether the freedom offered by Jesus can be "true" to the dual aspects of Christian liberation we have suggested in earlier chapters--the affirmation of selfhood and the concern that that selfhood be expressed as a vulnerability and concern for others; and whether this freedom--which we have seen is grounded in the friendship of Jesus--can empower women to be liberated and to speak in our own voices.

I have argued in the preceeding paragraphs that the freedom and authority grounded in the friendship of Jesus not only are "true" to both aspects of liberation we have affirmed earlier as Christian, but actually characterize that liberation in a more complete way. Thus I would suggest that the Christian community would be better described as a community characterized by its friendship and spontaneous freedom than as a community characterized by its service and altruism.[75]

Furthermore, I have suggested that the freedom and authority grounded in the friendship of Jesus would empower women to our liberation. The friends of Jesus are those who know--who are aware of--the liberating intention and activity of God, and who are then from the perspective of that knowledge to live both authoritatively and responsibly in the world. They are to live from their own centers and not according to an alien one, and they are called to live decisively as persons of responsibility. Inasmuch as women's bondage has been to live a life on the periphery that is characterized by responsiveness and submissiveness, the call to be Jesus' friends and to share in the authority, responsibility, and obligation of Jesus can, I would argue, be a liberating and empowering one for women today.[76]

NOTES

[1]See Chap II, p. 52.

[2]See Chap. IV, p.128.

[3]Dorothee Soelle, _Suffering_ (Philadelphia: Fortress Press, 1975), p. 11.

[4]Jürgen Moltmann, "The New Covenent of Freedom" in _The Power of the Powerless_ (London: SCM Press Ltd., 1981), p. 42.

[5]_Ibid._, p. 42.

[6]_Ibid._, p. 40.

[7]_Ibid._, p. 40.

[8]_Ibid._, p. 39.

[9]Delwin Brown, _To Set At Liberty: Christian Faith and Human Freedom_ (Maryknoll, New York: Orbis Books, 1981), p. 92.

[10]_Ibid._, p. 92.

[11]_Ibid._, p. 92.

[12]_Ibid._, p. 92.

[13]_Ibid._, p. 93.

[14]_Ibid._, p. 93.

[15]_Ibid._, p. 94.

[16]_Ibid._, p. 94.

[17]_Ibid._, p. 96.

[18]_Ibid._, p. 97.

[19]_Ibid._, p. 97.

[20]_Ibid._, p. 97.

[21]_Ibid._, p. 97.

[22]_Ibid._, p. 97.

[23]Ibid., p. 97.

[24]Ibid., p. 98.

[25]Ibid., p. 98.

[26]Ibid., p. 97.

[27]Ibid., p. 98.

[28]Ibid., p. 98.

[29]Ibid., p. 98.

[30]Ibid., p. 98.

[31]Ibid., p. 98.

[32]Ibid., p. 98.

[33]From "Doulous," by Karl Heinrich Rengstorf, found in Theological Dictionary of the New Testament, Vol. II, edited by Gerhard Kittel, translated by Geoffrey W. Bromily, Copyright 1964, Wm. B. Eerdmans Publishing Co., p. 261.

[34]Ibid., p. 261.

[35]Ibid., p. 261.

[36]Ibid., pp. 266-7.

[37]Ibid., p. 267.

[38]Ibid., p. 270.

[39]Ibid., p. 273.

[40]Ibid., p. 273.

[41]Ibid., p. 275.

[42]Ibid., p. 275.

[43]Ibid., pp. 275-76.

[44]Rudolf Bultmann, Theology of the New Testament vol. I (New York: Charles Scribner's Sons, 1951, 1955), p. 331.

[45]Ibid., p. 342.

[46]See Chapter II, p. 52.

[47]Romans 8:14-17. And, as Bultmann notes (p. 336), "to be 'led by the spirit' does not mean to be dragged along willy-nilly but directly presupposes decision in the alternatives: 'flesh' or 'Spirit.'"

[48]Rengstorf, p. 276.

[49]Ibid., p. 276.

[50]The Interpreter's Bible vol. VIII (New York: Abingdon-Cokesburg Press, 1952), Arthur John Gossip, exposition, p. 723.

[51]Ibid., p. 723.

[52]Ibid., p. 725.

[53]Ibid., p. 723.

[54]Ibid., p. 723.

[55]Ibid., p. 723.

[56]Ibid., p. 723.

[57]Dorothee Soelle, Beyond Mere Obedience (New York: The Pilgrim Press, 1982), p. xiii.

[58]Ibid., pp. xix-xx.

[59]Ibid., p. xx.

[60]Ibid., p. 23.

[61]Ibid., p. 24.

[62]Ibid., pp. 24-25.

[63]Ibid., p. 24.

[64]Ibid., p. 24. She adds that the obedient person however "remains a re-actor; he or she only fulfills that which is assigned; he is required to sacrifice his 'spontaneity' on the altar of obedience." Page 27.

[65]Ibid., p. 64.

[66]Ibid., p. 64.

[67]Ibid., p. 56.

[68]Ibid., p. 56.

[69]Ibid., p. 60.

[70]Jürgen Moltmann, The Passion for Life (Philadelphia: Fortress Press, 1978), trans., Douglas Meeks, p. 57.

[71]Ibid., p. 57.

[72]Ibid., p. 57.

[73]William Barclay, The Gospel of John, Vol. 2 (Philadelphia: The Westminster Press, 1956), p. 208. As Schüssler-Fiorenza has argued as well, Jesus as the incarnation of Sophia-God was one concerned with making people friends of God.

[74]Anne Carr seems to agree that friendship of God can be empowering when she asks: "What if God is friend to humanity as a whole, and even more intimately, friend to the individual, to me? A friend whose presence is joy, ever-deepening relationship and love, ever available in direct address, in communion and presence? A friend whose person is fundamentally a mystery, inexhaustible, never fully known, always surprising? Yet a friend, familiar, comforting, at home with us: a friend who urges our freedom and autonomy in decision, yet who is present in the community of interdependence and in fact creates it? A friend who widens our perspectives daily and who deepens our passion for freedom--our own and that of others? What if?" Anne Carr, "On Feminist Spirituality" Horizons 9 (Spring 1982), pp. 102-3.

[75]Elisabeth Schüssler-Fiorenza herself has suggested that the category of friend/friendship would be a good one for such a Christian community. In response to Mary Daly's use of the term "sisterhood of men" to describe the eschatalogical community, Schüssler-Fiorenza writes: "I wonder why the author never uses the category of friend/friendship which is not sex-stereotyped and

symbolizes a community of equals." in "Why Not the Category Friend/Friendship?" Horizons 2 1 (Spring 1975), pp. 117-18. Similarly, although "community of equals" is her predominant metaphor to describe the non-patriarchal Christian community, the notion of friendship is also evident in her work In Memory of Her. Just as she argues that in Scripture Sophia makes people friends of God, so she says, "In every generation Divine Wisdom commissions prophets--women and men--and makes them friends and children of God" (p. 345). And, in her discussion of the Gospel of John she calls the Johannine community a "community of friends" (pp. 323-25). Also, two books on friendship have recently been published: Janice Raymond's A Passion for Friends: Towards a Philosophy of Female Affections (Boston: Beacon Press, 1986) and Mary E. Hunt's Fierce Tenderness: Toward a Feminist Theology of Friendship (New York: Harper & Row, 1986).

[76]Anne Carr notes similarly that a feminist spirituality is one that "would encourage the autonomy, self-actualization, and self-transcendence of all women (and men). It would recognize the uniqueness of each individual as she tells her own story . . . and affirm each one as she strives to make her own choices. . . . Feminist spirituality would consciously struggle to free itself from ideologies in favor of the authentic freedom of the individual and the group as it attempts to be faithful to its own experience. . . . [it] would strive for an ever freer, but always human, self-transcendence before a God who does not call us servants but friends." "On Feminist Spirituality," p. 100.

EPILOGUE

The purpose of this book has been to discover whether Christianity can empower women to our liberation--to speak in our own voices. We have seen through our exploration of women's experience that women's liberation means our awareness of our bondage and our empowerment to name it as such and then to begin to name ouselves, speaking from our own centers--centers of integrity and authority--and in our own voices. Although not all women would affirm that women's process of liberation is divinely empowered at all, we have seen also that there are some women who would affirm that the liberation women experience is grounded in the call of God--a call that leads a woman to the awareness of her bondage and challenges/encourages her to take the risk of creating herself from her own center. This encouragement to name ourselves is more than a call, it is also a listening and empowering as the divine patiently hears us into our own speech.

And we have seen that the selfhood/authority/ freedom described by women's experience of liberation is one that is not described by a "cut-off-ness"--a state of autonomy where one lives only from and for oneself. Rather, the intuition is that women's selfhood is one formed through relationship and vulnerability. Rather than cut herself off from relationships, a woman forms her selfhood by making room for herself in the midst of these relationships, a space at the center as it were, from which she can distinguish her own voice from those of others and thus gain her own perspective/center from which she can then reintegrate them in her own way, speaking in her own voice. The freedom and selfhood women are affirming are deeply connected and vulnerable. Formed in response to others, her centered selfhood is fluid. Grounded in her own experience as she speaks her own story with her own voice, her authority reflects her newfound ability to integrate and spark others to discover their own authority.

We have heard as well the argument of Elisabeth Schüssler Fiorenza that Christianity can become a force for women's empowerment today. She has argued that the history of early Christian origins she has reconstructed is a story women can appropriate today. The history she recalls is of a gospel that is the call to move out of patriarchy into a

165

community of equals where there is no domination and where women have the opportunity to participate as equals in the decision-making processes. The story she tells is of women who heard this call and participated as leaders in this new community. Thus, she offers to women a gospel that points to a God beyond the boundaries of patriarchy who calls people to a new wholeness and a new liberation.

We have also seen that the liberation Schüssler-Fiorenza and Rosemary Ruether have suggested is a Christian liberation is characterized by a liberation to selfhood and wholeness which is expressed through service and altruism, the putting of the needs of others and the community first. Because this Christian liberation is one modified in this way, I have argued that it does not offer a liberation experience for women today. Rather, it effectively blocks women's liberation by reinforcing patterns of self-negation and attentiveness to others that are characteristic of women's experience under patriarchy.

However, through an exploration of the notions of service and altruism as they have theologically expressed the Christian affirmation of true liberation and true human fulfillment, we have discovered that service and altruism within the Christian context do not mean self-negation but the extension/shattering of an assumed self that it might live beyond itself in greater relationality and vulernability. Service and altruism reflect the Christian intuition that true human selfhood is one that is lived vulnerably and fluidly. Thus, I have argued that Christian liberation and wholeness mean not only service and altruism, but also the affirmation of self.

But because women's selfhood cannot be assumed, Christian liberation cannot be offered to women through the call to service and altruism. Thus we have explored the "prior-to" or "as-well-as" experience of Christian liberation characterized as a call to freedom. And I have argued that the freedom offered by Jesus is one that means a call to authority and selfhood. Moreover, the freedom and selfhood to which Jesus calls is an obligated, engaged freedom/selfhood. It is one that recognizes the claims of the neighbor upon itself and seeks from its own center of integrity, in the context of the knowledge of the intention of God revealed by Jesus, to create it own responsible response. The self created in this way is one that is created anew each moment as it responds to the world. It is a self for whom the caring and concern for the needs of others expressed in the notions of service and altruism are included in its freedom. If one accepts the freedom offered in Christianity, then one accepts it as the freedom to be a responsible self, creating oneself in the context of those around. This notion of freedom and selfhood, I have argued, includes the notion of service and altruism. Thus, I have suggested that the call to Christian liberation can be characterized as a call to freedom.

If the call to Christian liberation can be characterized as a call to freedom as explored here, can this call to freedom be a liberating call to women today? Can it call women to speak in our own voices? Because the call of Jesus is the call to respond from one's own center of authority and not according to an alien will, I have suggested that this call to freedom is one that can liberate women today. Jesus offers the knowledge that God is a God of liberation and empowerment and calls his followers to make this knowledge their own and to create their own responses, in the light of that knowledge, from their own centers. For women this would mean acknowledging our confinement under patriarchy and beginning to form our response from our own centers.

We have heard several reasons why Christianity cannot empower women today. It has been suggested that Christianity validates systems of patriarchal authority, making them seem to be the will of God "himself." Moreover, it has been argued that Christianity teaches women to be dependent upon male authority figures rather than calling us to trust ourselves. Thus women, it has been argued, cannot be liberated by Christianity.

However, we have seen through the arguments of Ruether and Schüssler-Fiorenza that Christianity is not necessarily patriarchal. Rather, when it is true to its proto-typical trajectory, Christianity is non-patriarchal and offers a tradition and a history of liberation that is usable against patriarchy today. Moreover, we have seen that Christian liberation is not about dependency upon male authority figures, but a call to form one's own

167

authority--to be one who knows and responds from one's own center of authority. Jesus offers his friends his own story--all he knows about God--all that he has experienced of the divine intent. He thus makes possible their own direct relationship with God. As such, Jesus encourages them not to be slaves, not to be dependent upon alien wills. Rather, Jesus calls them to hear what he has said, to make his story part of their own--woven together from their own centers of integrity--and then to create their own story. As Dorothee Soelle has suggested, Jesus does not demand of his friends mere obedience but asks of them a response--a response grounded in genuine concern for all, a response in the light of all that he has shared with them--yet a response that is truly and spontaneously their own. Thus what Christianity offers women is not dependency but friendship--a friendship which affirms that from deep within our own center of integrity we should begin to tell our own stories, singing them in our own voices.

This leads me to the conclusion that Christianity can empower women to be liberated--to speak in our own voices. Within the Christian tradition there is a source that can be used both against patriarchy and Christianity in its patriarchalized form and for the empowerment of women in our journey towards liberation. As women discover and reclaim this source, we call Christianity to return to its proto-typical trajectory away from patriarchy and towards a community of equals whose friendship with each other and toward the world can be a continual source for liberation today.

BIBLIOGRAPHY

Andolsen, Barbara Hilkert. "Agape in Feminist Ethics." The Journal of Religious Ethics 9 (Spring 1981): 69-81.

Barclay, William. The Gospel of John, vol. 2. Philadelphia: The Westminster Press, 1956.

Berger, Peter L. Pyramids of Sacrifice: Political Ethics and Social Change. New York: Basic Books, 1974.

Bernard, J. H. A Critical and Exegetical Commentary on the Gospel According to St. John, Vol. II. Edited by A. H. McNeile. Edinburgh: T & T Clark, 1928.

Brown, Delwin. To Set at Liberty: Christian Faith and Human Freedom. Maryknoll: Orbis Books, 1981.

Bultmann, Rudolf. Theology of the New Testament, Vol. 1. Translated by Kendrick Grobel. New York: Charles Scribner's Sons, 1951.

Carr, Anne. "On Feminist Spirituality." Horizons 9 (Spring 1982), pp. 96-103.

Chodorow, Nancy. The Reproduction of Mothering: Psychoanalysis and the Sociology of Gender. Berkeley: University of California Press, 1978.

Christ, Carol P. "Another Response to a Religion for Women." WomanSpirit, Summer Solstice 1980, Vol. 6 #24, pp. 27-29.

_____. "Why Women Need the Goddess: Phenomenological, Psychological, and Political Reflections." In The Politics of Women's Spirituality: Essays on the Rise of Spiritual Power Within the Feminist Movement. Edited by Charlene Spretnak. Garden City: Anchor Press/Doubleday, 1982, pp. 71-86.

Christ, Carol P. and Plaskow, Judith, ed. WomanSpirit Rising: A Feminist Reader in Religion, 1979.

Clark, Elizabeth and Richardson, Herbert, ed. Women and Religion: A Feminist Sourcebook of Christian Thought. New York: Harper & Row, 1977.

Collins, Sheila D. A Different Heaven and Earth.

Valley Forge: Judson Press, 1974.

Cone, James H. Black Theology and Black Power. New York: The Seabury Press, 1969.

_____. My Soul Looks Back. Nashville: Abingdon, 1982.

Daly, Mary. Beyond God the Father: Toward a Philosophy of Women's Liberation. Boston: Beacon Press, 1973.

_____. The Church and the Second Sex. New York: Harper Colophon, 1975.

_____. Gyn/Ecology: The Metaphysics of Radical Feminism. Boston: Beacon Press, 1984.

_____. Pure Lust: Elemental Feminist Philosophy. Boston: Beacon Press, 1984.

de Beauvoir, Simone. The Second Sex. Translated by H. M. Parshley. New York: Vintage Books/Random House, 1974; Gallimard, 1949.

Dinnerstein, Dorothy. The Mermaid and the Minotaur: Sexual Arrangements and Human Malaise. New York: Harper Colophon, 1977.

Doely, Sarah Bentley, ed. Women's Liberation and the Church: The New Demand for Freedom in the Life of the Christian Church. New York: Association Press, 1970.

Dunfee, Susan Nelson. "The Sin of Hiding: A Feminist Critique of Reinhold Niebuhr's Account of the Sin of Pride." Soundings (Fall 1982): 316-327.

Fairchild, Roy. "Spiritual Guidance in Ego-Strengthening Experience," paper presented at Schaff Lectures at Pittsburgh Theological Seminary, Spring 1983.

Feuerbach, Ludwig. The Essence of Christianity. Translated by George Eliot. New York: Harper Torchbooks/Harper & Row, 1957.

Filson, Floyd V. The Layman's Bible Commentary: The Gospel According to John, Vol. 19. Richmond: John Knox Press, 1963.

170

Fiorenza, Elisabeth Schüssler. In Memory of Her: A Feminist Theological Reconstruction of Christian Origins. New York: Crossroad, 1983.

_____. "Why Not the Category of Friend/Friendship?" Horizons (Spring 1975): 117-18.

Freire, Paulo. Pedagogy of the Oppressed. Translated by Myra Bergman Ramos. New York: A Continuum Book/The Seabury Press, 1970.

Friedrich, Gerhard, ed. Theological Dictionary of the New Testament. Vol. IX. Grand Rapids: Eerdmans Publishing Co., 1974.

Gilligan, Carol. In a Different Voice: Psychological Theory and Women's Development. Cambridge: Harvard University Press, 1982.

Goldenberg, Naomi. Changing of the Gods: Feminism and the End of Traditional Religions. Boston: Beacon Press, 1979.

Gould, Carol C., ed. Beyond Domination: New Perspectives on Women and Philosophy. Totowa, N.J.: Rowman & Allanheld, 1983.

Gray, Elizabeth Dodson. Green Paradise Lost. Wellesley, MA: Roundtable Press, 1981.

Griffin, Susan. Pornography and Silence: Culture's Revenge Against Nature. New York: Harper & Row, 1981.

Gutierrez, Gustavo. A Theology of Liberation: History, Politics, and Salvation. Translated by Sister Caridad Inda and John Eagleson. Maryknoll: Orbis Books, 1973.

Harder, Sarah. "The Wife I Wasn't Meant to Be." Redbook, February 1973, pp. 40-44.

Harrison, Beverly Wildung. Our Right to Choose: Toward a New Ethic of Abortion. Boston: Beacon Press, 1983.

_____. "The Power of Anger in the Work of Love: Christian Ethics for Women and Other Persons." Union Seminary Quarterly Review 36 (supplementary issue 1981): 41-43, 54-57.

Hastings, Edward, ed. The Speaker's Bible: The Gospel According to St. John, Vol. II. Grand Rapids: Baker Book House, 1962.

Heyward, Isabel Carter. The Redemption of God: A Theology of Mutual Relation. New York: University Press of America, 1982.

Interpreter's Bible, Vol. VIII "Exposition on the Gospel of John," by Arthur John Gossip. New York: Abingdon-Cokesbury Press, 1952.

Keller, Catherine E. "From a Broken Web: Sexism, Separation, and Self." Ph.D. dissertation, Claremont Graduate School, 1982.

_____. From a Broken Web: Separation, Sexism, and Self. Boston: Beacon Press, 1986.

Miller, Jean Baker. Toward a New Psychology of Women. Boston: Beacon Press, 1976.

Moltmann, Jürgen. The Passion for Life. Translated by Douglas Meeks. Philadelphia: Fortress Press, 1978.

_____. The Power of the Powerless. Translated by Margaret Kohl. London: SCM Press Ltd., 1981.

Moltmann-Wendel, Elisabeth. Liberty, Equality, Sisterhood: On the Emancipation of Women in Church and Society. Translated by Ruth Gritsch. Philadelphia: Fortress Press, 1978.

Moltmann-Wendel, Elisabeth and Moltmann, Jürgen. "Becoming Human in New Community." In The Community of Women and Men in the Church, pp. 29-42. Edited by Constance F. Parvey. Philadelphia: Fortress Press, 1983.

Morgan, Robin. The Anatomy of Freedom: Feminism, Physics, and Global Politics. Garden City: Anchor Press/Doubleday, 1982.

Niebuhr, Reinhold. Faith and History: A Comparison of Christian and Modern Views of History. New York: Charles Scribner's Sons, 1949.

_____. The Nature and Destiny of Man: A Christian Interpretation, Vol. I: Human Nature. New York: Charles Scriber's Sons, 1964.

172

_____. The Nature and Destiny of Man: A Christian Interpretation, Vol. II: Human Destiny. New York: Charles Scribner's Sons, 1964.

Ohanneson, Joan. Woman: Survivor in the Church. Minneapolis: Winston Press, 1980.

Outka, Gene. Agape: An Ethical Analysis. New Haven: Yale University Press, 1972.

Plaskow, Judith. Sex, Sin and Grace: Women's Experience and the Theologies of Reinhold Niebuhr and Paul Tillich. Washington, D.C.: University Press of America, 1980.

Rich, Adrienne. A Wild Patience Has Taken Me This Far. New York: W. W. Norton & Co., 1981.

_____. The Dream of a Common Language. New York: W. W. Norton & Co., 1978.

Ruether, Rosemary Radford. Liberation Theology. New York: Paulist Press, 1972.

_____. New Woman New Earth: Sexist Ideologies and Human Liberation New York: A Crossroad Book/The Seabury Press, 1975.

_____. "A Religion for Women." WomanSpirit, Summer Solstice 1980, pp. 22-25.

_____. "Sexism and the Theology of Liberation." The Christian Century, December 12, 1973, pp. 1224-1229.

_____. Sexism and God-Talk: Toward a Feminist Theology. Boston: Beacon Press, 1983.

Ruether, Rosemary Radford, ed. Religion and Sexism: Images of Woman in the Jewish and Christian Traditions. New York: Simon & Schuster, 1974.

Russell, Letty M. Human Liberation in a Feminist Perspective--A Theology. Philadelphia: The Westminster Press, 1974.

Saiving, Valerie. "The Human Situation: A Feminist View." In WomanSpirit Rising, pp. 25-42. Edited by Christ and Plaskow. San Francisco: Harper & Row, 1979. Originally published in Journal of Religion,

40 (April, 1960) by the University of Chicago Press,
Copyright 1960, The University of Chicago.

Scanzoni, Letha and Hardesty, Nancy, ed. All We're
Meant to Be. Waco, Texas: Word Books, 1974.

Schaef, Anne Wilson. Women's Reality: An Emerging
Female System in the White Male Society.
Minneapolis: Winston Press, 1981.

Silverstein, Shel. The Giving Tree. New York:
Harper & Row, 1964.

Soelle, Dorothee. Beyond Mere Obedience. Translated
by Lawrence W. Denef. New York: The Pilgrim Press,
1982.

_____. Suffering. Translated Everett R. Kalin.
Philadelphia: Fortress Press, 1975.

Spretnak, Charlene, ed. The Politics of Women's
Spirituality: Essays on the Rise of Spiritual Power
Within the Feminist Movement. Garden City: Anchor
Books, 1982.

Steinem, Gloria. "Ruth's Song (Because She Could Not
Sing It)." In Outrageous Acts and Everyday
Rebellions, pp. 129-146. New York: Holt, Rinehart
and Winston, 1983.

Suchocki, Marjorie Hewitt. God Christ Church: A
Practical Guide to Process Theology. New York:
Crossroad, 1982.

Theological Dictionary of the New Testament, Vol. II,
edited by Gerhard Kittel, translated by Geoffrey W.
Bromiley, Copyright 1964, Wm. B. Eerdmans Publishing
Co. S.v., "Doulous," by Karl Heinrich Rengstrof.

Tillich, Paul. Love, Power, and Justice: Ontological
Analyses and Ethical Applications. New York: Oxford
University Press, 1954.

Trible, Phyllis. God and the Rhetoric of Sexuality.
Philadelphia: Fortress Press, 1978.

Walker, Alice. The Color Purple. New York:
Washington Square Press, 1982.

Williams, Daniel Day. God's Grace and Man's Hope.

New York: Harper & Brothers, 1949.

_____. <u>The Spirit and the Forms of Love</u>.
Washington, DC: University Press of America, 1981.

Woolf, Virginia. <u>A Room of One's Own</u>. New York:
Harcourt Brace Jovanovich, 1957.